George E. Cokayne

State of the Peerage of Ireland

at and Since the Time of the Union 1801 to 1888 - Also, list of the Knights

of St. Patrick, at and since the institution of that order, 1783 to 1888

George E. Cokayne

State of the Peerage of Ireland
*at and Since the Time of the Union 1801 to 1888 - Also, list of the Knights of St.
Patrick, at and since the institution of that order, 1783 to 1888*

ISBN/EAN: 9783337284534

Printed in Europe, USA, Canada, Australia, Japan

Cover: Foto ©Andreas Hilbeck / pixelio.de

More available books at **www.hansebooks.com**

STATE OF THE

Peerage of Ireland,

AT AND SINCE THE TIME OF THE UNION

1801 to 1888.

ALSO

List of the Knights of St. Patrick,

AT AND SINCE THE INSTITUTION OF THAT ORDER,

1783 to 1888.

EDITED BY

G. E. Cokayne

From *The Genealogist* (New Series) vol. v, 1888, ed. by W. D. Selby
LONDON : GEORGE BELL AND SONS.
EXETER : WILLIAM POLLARD & Co., PRINTERS, NORTH STREET.
1889.

The Peerage of Ireland.

SOME REMARKS ON ITS STATE AT AND SINCE THE UNION, 1ST JANUARY 1801,

TOGETHER WITH AN APPENDIX CONTAINING THE FOLLOWING TABLES,

VIZ. :—

TABLE I. Peerages[1] existing at the time of the Union (1 Jan. 1801), arranged *according to their precedence*, and continued to the present date (31 Dec. 1887), showing not only the names and the number of each rank existing at those two periods, but also those who *then* held, or *now* hold, an hereditary Peerage in the House of Lords, together with those who at the present date (being 88 in all) are Peers of Ireland *alone.*

TABLE II. Peerages[1] existing at the time of the Union, of which the creation was *anterior* to the accession of George III (the then reigning monarch) ; arranged (chronologically) *according to the date of the most ancient peerage* enjoyed by the then Peer.

TABLE III. Peerages[1] which at the time of the Union were held, *suo jure*, by Females ; arranged *according to their precedence.*

TABLE IV. Peerages[1] extinct since the date of the Union, shewing the extinction of *all* peerages held by *the same* person, of which the patents were *distinct ;* arranged chronologically.

TABLE V. Peerages[1] which existed *separately* at the time of the Union, but which have since *merged* into higher or more ancient titles ; arranged chronologically.

TABLE VI. Peerages[1] *created* since the Union, with the names of the three Peerages on whose extinction they were created in accordance with the Act of the Union ; arranged chronologically.

TABLE VII. "Promotions" (*i.e.* Peerages[1] conferred on those who already held a Peerage) made since the Union ; arranged chronologically.

TABLE VIII. Peerages[1] which at the time of the Union were united with Peerages of England or of Great Britain ; as also Peerages[1] which since that date have become united therewith or with Peerages of the United Kingdom ; arranged chronologically in the order of such their Union.

TABLE IX. List of Irish Representative Peers since the Union ; arranged chronologically.

TABLE X. List of the Knights of the Order of St. Patrick from the institution of that Order, 5 Feb., 1783.

INDEX to the title of each Peerage and the surname of each Peer mentioned in the above Tables.

Had the Union between the Kingdoms of Great Britain and Ireland been carried out (as was the case in the Union with Scotland), without any *special* power having been retained for creating (or "promoting") any Irish Peerage, such creations (or "promotions") would *ipso facto* have come to an end, when there no longer existed a separate KINGDOM OF IRELAND, to which such future peerages could refer, but only *one* Kingdom, *viz.*, that of the UNITED KINGDOM *of Great Britain and Ireland.* In this way the creation of Peers of GREAT BRITAIN, which by the Irish Union no longer existed as a *separate* kingdom, *did* actually at that date so terminate. *But* for such special (and most undesirable)

---

[1] All Peerages spoken of in this article are to be considered as Peerages *of the Kingdom of Ireland* unless otherwise specified.

power, the number of Irish Peers without *hereditary* seats in the House of Lords would at this time (1887) have been but 76, in lieu of 88,[1] or, deducting the 28 Representative Peers, 48 in lieu of 60.[1] This result, however, was prevented by the then Monarch (George III) insisting upon retaining the (since the Union) useless and hurtful prerogative of creating Peers of a Kingdom that had ceased separately to exist. The matter ended in a compromise between the King and the Ministry, whereby *special clauses* were introduced in the Act for the Union to enable the Crown *to continue* under certain limitations, *the creation* and "promotion" of *Irish Peerages*; which clauses, being at once obscure in themselves and pernicious in their tendency, have, it is trusted, a fair prospect of being shortly repealed.

In the "Gentleman's Magazine" for October and November 1855, are two articles by the late Mr. John Gough Nichols, its accomplished Editor, (relating especially to the then recent creation of the Barony of Fermoy, hereafter alluded to) which articles put the whole matter, as to the power reserved for the creation and "promotion" of Irish Peerages after the Union, in a very clear light. Free use is here made of both these articles and the following is an extract therefrom :—

"The Fourth Article of Union between the Kingdoms of Great Britain and Ireland contains the regulations under which the Peers of Ireland were in future to sit in parliament, and under which the Crown was to 'create peers of that part of the United Kingdom, and to make promotions in the peerage thereof.'

'To make promotions in the peerage thereof '—an expression certainly inappropriate and incongruous when viewed with eyes that have studied in the pages of Dugdale, Cruise, and Nicolas. It looks as if it had emanated from the War Office or the Admiralty, rather than the College of Arms. When a Captain is promoted to a Majority he ceases to be a Captain, when a Major is promoted to a Lieutenant-Colonelcy he ceases to be a Major, and when a Colonel becomes a general officer he is no longer styled Colonel,—though then, and never till then, he may be Colonel of a regiment. But when a Baron is made a Viscount he does not lose his Barony ; when an Earl is raised to a Marquessate he is both a Marquess and an Earl ; and when a Marquess is elevated to the highest grade of the peerage he still retains all the accumulated dignities that may have descended to him from his ancestors, or that have been previously conferred upon himself.

However, the Act of Union declared —

'That it shall be lawful for his Majesty, his heirs and successors, to create Peers of that part of the United Kingdom called Ireland, and *to make promotions in the peerage thereof*, after the Union ;'

and upon the authority of those few words, which we have here printed in the italic character, the successive advisers of the Crown during the present century have acted very largely. The so-called 'promotions' in the peerage of Ireland have been made without stint, *mero motu* of the Crown ; whilst the 'new creations,' understanding by that expression the elevation of *commoners* to the peerage, have been limited, in pursuance of the stipulations of the same articles of Union, to one new peerage in lieu of every three that became extinct. In order to show the whole law in this matter we here introduce the entire clause which belongs to this subject :

'That it shall be lawful for his Majesty, his heirs and successors, to create Peers of that part of the United Kingdom called Ireland, and to make promotions in the peerage thereof, after the Union ; provided that no new creation of any such peerage shall take place after the Union until three of the peerages of Ireland which shall

---

[1] *i.e.*, the difference caused by the twelve Peers (possessing Peerages of Ireland *alone*) created *since* the Union - viz., the Earl of Norbury, the Viscounts Gort and Guillamore and the Barons Rendlesham, Castlemaine, Decies, Garvagh, Oranmore, Dunsandle, Bellew, Fermoy and Rathdonnel. This is independent of *eight* other creations since the Union, of whom four obtained Peerages in the United Kingdom, while four others have become extinct. See Tables VI, VIII and IX.

have been existing at the time of the Union shall have become extinct; and upon such extinction of three peerages it shall be lawful for his Majesty, his heirs and successors, to create one Peer of that part of the United Kingdom called Ireland; and in like manner so often as three peerages of that part of the United Kingdom called Ireland shall become extinct, it shall be lawful for his Majesty, his heirs and successors, to create one other Peer of the said part of the United Kingdom; and if it shall happen that the Peers of that part of the United Kingdom called Ireland shall by extinction of peerages or otherwise, be reduced to the number of one hundred, exclusive of all such Peers of that part of the United Kingdom called Ireland as shall hold any peerage of Great Britain subsisting at the time of the Union, or of the United Kingdom created since the Union, by which such Peers shall be entitled to an hereditary seat in the House of Lords of the United Kingdom, then and in that case it shall and may be lawful for his Majesty, his heirs and successors, to create one Peer of that part of the United Kingdom called Ireland as often as any one of such one hundred peerages shall fail by extinction, or as often as any one Peer of that part of the United Kingdom called Ireland shall become entitled by descent or creation to an hereditary seat in the House of Lords of the United Kingdom; it being the true intent and meaning of this article that at all times after the Union it shall and may be lawful for his Majesty, his heirs and successors, to keep up the peerage of that part of the United Kingdom called Ireland to the number of one hundred, over and above the number of any such Peers as shall be entitled by descent or creation to an hereditary seat in the House of Lords of the United Kingdom.'

The next clause enacts that peerages in abeyance shall be deemed existing peerages and that no peerage shall be deemed extinct but on default of claim for a year after the death of the late possessor—the claim to be made in such form and manner as the House of Lords from time to time may prescribe. If after that, or a longer period, a claim be made and allowed, and a new creation shall have taken place in the interval, it is enacted that no new right of creation shall accrue to the Crown on the next extinction of a peerage.''

L "Peerage." With respect to what the framers of the Union Act meant by the term "*Peerages of Ireland existing at the time of the Union*" (no explanation being vouchsafed in the Act itself,) there are at least four different ways of explaining it. (1). The most reasonable interpretation seems to be that which (excepting in the Fermoy case, hereafter alluded to) has been adopted—viz., that *all* Peerages held by one and the same person at the time of the Union should be held as but *one* Peerage. (2). It may be held to mean that all Peerages so held, of which the *remainders* were *different*, should be reckoned as *distinct* Peerages. (3). That all Peerages so held, which were conferred by *different patents* (or other modes of creation) should be reckoned as *distinct* Peerages. (4). It *may* be held (though it hardly could be sustained) that any number of Peerage titles, if of different grade, should, though conferred in the *same* patent, be reckoned as *distinct* Peerages.—Take, for example, the case of the extinction of the Peerage of Clermont, which was as follows: At the time of the Union, William Henry Fortescue was possessed of the Earldom of Clermont (1777) of the Viscountcy and Barony of Clermont, conferred together (1776) with a special remainder, and also of a more ancient (1770) Barony of Clermont. According to the first way of interpreting the Act, he possessed but *one* Peerage; according to the second way (the remainder of the Viscountcy &c., being distinct from that of the Earldom) he possessed *two* Peerages; according to the third way (having three Peerages with distinct patents) he possessed *three* Peerages; while, according to the fourth way (having one Earldom, one Viscountcy and two distinct Baronies) he possessed *four* Peerages. When he died without male issue, in 1806, the Earldom and the older Barony (1770) became extinct, but the Viscountcy and Barony (1776) continued. Accordingly such extinction was not acted upon, as to the creation of a new Peer, according to the first (and most rational) interpretation of what was meant by the Union Act, as applied to such cases. The *reverse*, however, of this interpretation was sought to be established by the extinctions used for the creation of the Barony of Fermoy, which was endeavoured to be effected as follows:

11. THE FERMOY CASE. In 1855, Edmund Burke Roche, of Trabolgan, co. Cork, M.P. for that county, was gazetted as having been raised to the Irish Peerage under the title of Baron Fermoy; the three extinctions made use of for that creation (under the special clause in the Union Act) being (1) Tyrconnel, (2) Melbourne (to which two there could be no objection) and (3) Mountrath. Now the Earldom of Mountrath had become extinct as far back as 1802, the Barony of Castle Coote, which was held by the *same* person at the time of the Union, remaining. The extinction of this Earldom was the first of a similar nature that had occurred since the Union, and was evidently made use of here as the forerunner for the introduction of a similar use to be made of the many subsequent ones. (See Table iv.) Accordingly, on the 24th July 1855, the Earl of Derby brought the matter before the House of Lords in a memorable speech commencing with the words "An Irishman, of the name of Roche, &c." Earl Granville, on behalf of the Government, undertook "not to advise Her Majesty to make use of any further exercise of her Prerogative in this way before the meeting of the next Session of Parliament." Lord Fermoy's claim to vote (at the election of Irish Representative Peers) in right of his (informal) creation was then referred to the Judges thus, *viz.*, "Was the extinction of the Earldom of Mountrath an extinction of a Peerage of Ireland according to the true construction of the Act of Union?" Decision was given on 19 May 1856, two (*viz.*, Mr. Justice Willes and Mr. Baron Bramwell) out of the ten Judges holding that it *was*, while the remaining eight (*viz.*, Lord Chief Baron Pollock, Mr. Baron Alderson, and Mr. Justices Coleridge, Cresswell, Erle, Wightman, Williams, and Crowder) held it was *not*; the Chief Baron backing up his opinion with the remark that such was "the exposition which the statute has received in the construction put upon it by a practice of half a century." Accordingly, a year (as required by the Union Act) having elapsed since the extinction (12 Feb. 1855) of the Viscountcy of O'Neill, *that* Peerage was substituted for the Earldom of Mountrath, and my Lord Fermoy received another patent of Peerage, dated 10 Sep. 1856, founded on the extinctions of (1) Tyrconnel (2) Melbourne and (3) O'Neill. The slipshod language of the Act of Union and the constant confusion therein of the words "Peers" and "Peerage" was severely commented on by several of the Judges. It is curious that the only instances (but three in all) in which the right of the Crown to confer a Peerage has been questioned, have arisen out of the construction to be put on the respective Acts of Union (Scotland and Ireland) *viz.*, as to Scotland in the cases of the Dukedom of Brandon (1711) and the Dukedom of Dover (1719) and, as to Ireland, in the case (1855) of the Barony of Fermoy. The right of the Crown to create Peerages, in the kingdom over which it reigns, to an *unlimited* extent, being so clear, it seems extraordinary that at the time of the Irish Union any value should have been attached

by the then King for the passing of a clause to enable it to create, to a *limited* extent, the anomalous dignity of a separate Peerage for a kingdom which, like Ireland after the Union, had no separate existence.[1]

III. "PROMOTIONS." With regard to the words "to make PROMOTIONS in the Peerage thereof" it seems very doubtful whether the proviso, that "no new creation" should take place until there were three extinctions, does not apply to this power of "promotion" *i.e.*, the raising (by creation) an existing *Peer* to a higher grade in the Peerage (which is of course the meaning, though an incorrect one, of the word "*promotion*") as well as to the raising a *Commoner* to the Peerage. Both can only be accomplished by the *creation* of a new Irish Peerage, and, in point of fact, each one of all the "promotions" that have been made has accordingly been effected by a *bonâ fide* patent of a *new* Irish Peerage, such patent resembling, in all respects, the one used for the creation of a Commoner, and such Peerage in no way interfering with the Irish title held previously by the grantee; *e.g.*, when in 1822 the then Viscount Monck was *cr.* (by promotion) Earl of Rathdown (which Earldom became extinct at his death, 1848), he still retained his former Peerage, which still (1887) exists. How then can the Viscountcy of Monck (which still exists in its *former* state) be said to have been "promoted"? The effect of "promotion" is to create a new Irish *Peerage*, though not a new Irish *Peer*. The illegality of "*promotions*," excepting under the special powers enabling the Crown to make "*creations*," was apparently held by the Law Advisers of the Crown during the long period from 1831 to 1868 when none were made. But in 1868, the legal world was somewhat startled—not at the Marquess of

---

[1] The power of the Crown as to the creation of any dignity is absolute. It is not however *retrospective :* the Crown cannot, for instance, create a *separate* Peerage of the kingdom of England, of Scotland, or of Great Britain, inasmuch as none of those kingdoms now *separately* exist (any more than the kingdom of Mercia) but are absorbed in that of the "United Kingdom." So, but for the special clause in the Union Act, would it have been as to the Peerage of Ireland.

Although as to the creation of Peers, the Crown cannot do what is impossible (*i.e.* cannot, save in this instance. owing to the anomalous clause in an Act of Parliament so enabling it, create a separate Peerage for a kingdom that has no separate existence) it can confer Peerages in any manner of ways and with any manner of limitations, *e.g.* for life, or, probably, even for a less estate, or *(per contra)* with any imaginable remainder. The right to a *seat in the House of Lords* is, however, another matter, and, unless there is a remainder in favour of some line of heirs, such right is not conceded by that house. Such was the case of Sir James Parke, created, 16 Jan. 1856, Baron Wensleydale, *for life*, who was excluded from the House of Lords till his Peerage was regranted him with the usual limitation. It appears also that the Peerage in which a Peer has once sat cannot (by the rules of that House) be taken from him, as was held in the case of the Barony of Buckhurst in which the present Earl Delawarr sat for many years in the House of Lords, and of which he was held *not* to be divested, notwithstanding that it ought (according to a wonderful but somewhat unintelligible shifting clause contained in the patent of its creation) to have devolved, when its owner became Earl Delawarr, on *somebody* else.

Many peers, however, have sat in the House of Lords in right of a Peerage of which the remainder has not been to the heir male of their body *e.g.* the Duke of Somerset in 1547, the Earl Vane in 1823 (the remainder being in both cases, primarily, to their second son), the Viscount Campden in 1628, the Earl of Feversham in 1676 (their Peerages being for life only with rem. to their respective sons in law), &c. There is also the case of Lord Hyde, whose Peerage (1756) was with rem. to his issue male by his then wife, with rem. to such wife and the heirs male of *her* body.

Abercorn receiving a Dukedom (for that reward his services had doubtless well merited) but that such Dukedom should be one in the Kingdom of Ireland, effected (in a way always of *doubtful* legality and *at that time* almost *obsolete*) by "promotion" of his Irish Viscountcy of Strabane.

It is to be observed that the number of "promotions" made since the Union is 29, of which but two have been made since 1825—viz., the Earldom of Ranfurly, by William IV, in 1831, and the Dukedom of Abercorn, in 1868, as abovementioned. The principle on which "promotions" have been conducted has been that as far as the remainder of the newly-created Peerage went, it should follow, and in no case exceed, the remainder of the (old) Peerage "promoted." Thus, when in 1827, John (Toler), Baron Norbury, was created Earl of Norbury, with a *special* remainder (*i.e.*, one to his second son) it was very properly considered a new creation and not a "promotion," the remainder of the new Peerage, though *within* the limits of the Barony of Norbury, not being identical therewith. On his death, in July 1831, his dignities branched out into two separate Irish Peerages enjoyed by (his two sons) two distinct persons, though it so happened that the next year, by the death of the elder of his sons, who was unmarried, they coalesced.

IV. NEW CREATIONS. Bad as was the expedient of creating *one* Irish Peerage for every *three* extinctions,[1] even this gradual reduction would in the course of time have perceptibly diminished, or even actually extinguished this (after the Union) anomalous order; but worse remained behind, for the Act goes on to declare that, when the number of Irish Peers was reduced to 100 "exclusive of all such Peers of that part of the United Kingdom called Ireland as shall hold any Peerage of Great Britain subsisting at the time of the Union, or of the United Kingdom created since the Union, by which such Peers shall be entitled to an Hereditary Seat in the House of Lords," it shall be lawful to create one "*Peer*," "as often as any one of such 100 *Peerages* shall fail by extinction," or as often as any "*Peer*" acquires an Hereditary Seat in the House of Lords by creation or inheritance; so as to ensure [what certainly is a most undesirable object] the keeping up the number of Irish Peers, *not* entitled to such Hereditary Seat, to 100. It is difficult to arrive at the precise meaning of this clause, as according to the first part all Irish Peers who possess *English* Peerages (as distinct from Peerages of Great Britain or of the United Kingdom) such as the Earls of Waterford and Desmond, the Viscounts Grandison, Lumley, &c. (who, in England, are Earls of Shrewsbury, Denbigh, Jersey, Scarbrough, &c.), would be *included* in the 100, while, according to the latter part of the clause (inasmuch as they have Hereditary Seats in the House of Lords) they would be *excluded*.

Some few years ago, the number of Irish Peers, who possessed no Peerage either in *England*, Great Britain, or Ireland, was reduced to 100, reckoning among such some few (about whose *right* to the Peerage there can be but little doubt) who have not established their claim to the

---

[1] Such extinctions were confined to those of Peerages *existing* at the time of the Union, so that the extinction of a Peerage like that of Fitzgerald and Vesey (created *after* the Union) which happened in 1860 did not reckon among them. There was also no account taken of any merger of which, since the Union, there have been several.—See Table V.

Peerage, *e.g.,* " Valentia," " Sherard,",&c. The number of such Peers in 1887 is but 88, no new creations having been made since 1868.

V. THE GRADUAL ABSORPTION OF SCOTCH AND IRISH PEERS. It is much to be hoped that the special powers of creating Irish Peerages as given by the Union Act will be altogether repealed, and the Peerage left (as that of Scotland) to the effect of time, when the anomaly of its *separate* existence will gradually become less marked, until by extinction or absorption it altogether ceases. In 1875, Lord Inchiquin (who was not only *a* Representative Peer of Ireland, but *the* representative of one of the most illustrious houses of that Kingdom—that of O'Brien, Earls, Marquesses, and sometime Princes and Kings of Thomond)—took the matter in hand. Having obtained from the Crown a reply to an Address from Parliament, in which the Sovereign declared "that the Powers reserved by the Act of Union of making creations and promotions in the Peerage of Ireland" should not stand in the way of Parliament considering the subject, his Lordship brought forward an Act for the approval of the next Session, entitled "The Irish Peerage Act, 1876," repealing so much of the Acts "for the Union of Great Britain and Ireland as authorises Her Majesty, her heirs and successors, to create[1] Peers of that part of the United Kingdom called Ireland." The original scheme contained other clauses, *e.g.,* to increase the number of Representative Peers in Ireland (the Irish Bishops having been deprived of their seats in the House of Lords), &c., but the above was all that passed the House of Lords, who sent it down as early as the 9th May to the House of Commons. Here, unfortunately, it was not proceeded with till very late in the Session, and consequently (in the hurry and turmoil of the last days thereof) failed to become law ; the House having been " counted out " during its last reading, owing to an Irishman and " Home Ruler," Sir John McKenna, M.P. for Youghal, having moved " to report progress." A measure, however, such as this, is absolutely necessary, as the *foundation* of any reform to be made in the present anomalous state of the Irish Peerage, inasmuch as it stops the *perpetuation* of the abuse. It would, however, be more desirable that any bill brought forward on the subject should deal with the Peerage of Scotland, as well as with that of Ireland, and should be of such a nature as would deal with the whole matter of all Peerages not possessing Hereditary Seats in the House of Lords, and, once for all, settle it finally.

Some such enactments as the following would *gradually* and without causing at any one time any perceptible increase in the House of Lords absorb the anomalous body of Peers excluded from the chief privilege of the Peerage :—

1. "That no creations be made of Irish Peers, under the enabling clauses of the Act of Union."

2. "That every person *hereafter* elected a Representative Peer for Scotland should (as in the case of Ireland) retain his seat for life."

---

[1] This would doubtless include the "*promotions*" therein authorized—they being (as before was observed) *actual creations of new Peerages,* though conferred only on those who already possess a Peerage of the same Kingdom.

3. " That to every Peerage of Scotland or Ireland, in which any person *(hereafter* elected a Representative Peer) shall have taken his seat, there shall be attached an *hereditary* seat in the House of Lords; the rank and precedence of such Peerage in such House, as elsewhere, continuing the same as heretofore, under the respective Acts of Union."

The effect of this would be that, on the death of any (future elected) Representative Peer, his successor would succeed to a Peerage entitling him to a (hereditary) seat in the House of Lords, while there would be, by such death, a vacancy among the Representative Peers, which vacancy, when filled up, would cause an increase of *one* to such House; this increase would, however, come to an end when the number of persons capable of being elected Representative Peers was in Scotland under 16, and in Ireland under 28. Such increase (allowing for future extinctions and for future creations of Scotch or Irish Peers to a Peerage of the United Kingdom) would, probably, in all not exceed 50 persons, and would take some 50 years or more to accomplish.

In the Peerages of Scotland and Ireland there is yet another anomaly, which (though by no means of equal moment to the above) might as well be remedied. It is this—a great many of these Peers, known (and *ranked*) in the House of Lords (and there only) under the title of some obscure Barony (such as Lord Saltersford, Lord Fisherwick, and Lord Sundridge), are elsewhere known as an earl, a marquess, and even a duke, and actually enjoy such higher precedence. This anomaly, which the above proposed enactments would in a great measure remedy, could be *entirely* got rid of in the same gradual manner, if, in the same Act, it were enacted—

" That at any time hereafter when the number of persons capable of being elected representative Peers shall in Scotland be under 16, or in Ireland under 28, it shall be lawful to elect a representative Peer from among such Peers of each such respective kingdom as may possess a Peerage in England, Great Britain, or the United Kingdom (in addition to their Scotch or Irish Peerage), exclusive, however, of any Peer who, *under this Act*, has inherited an hereditary seat in the House of Lords."

Thus, the Marquess of Sligo, if so elected, would sit in the House, as would his successors, according to the precedence of the Irish Marquess-ate of Sligo, and not (as at present) according to that of the Barony of Monteagle in the United Kingdom.

G. E. C.

APPENDIX.

Note.—In these tables the abbreviations "*cr.*," "*ex.*," "*merg.*," and "*pr.*," are used respectively for "*created*," "*extinct*," "*merged*," and "*promoted*." The letters "E.," "G.B.," and "U.K.," stand respectively for "ENGLAND," "GREAT BRITAIN," and the "UNITED KINGDOM."

TABLE I.

PEERAGES EXISTING AT THE TIME OF THE UNION (1 JANUARY 1801),

arranged *according to their precedence,* and continued to the present date (31 Dec. 1887) shewing not only the names and the number of each rank existing at those two periods, but also those who *then* held or *now* hold an Hereditary *Peerage in the House of Lords* (such Peerages being marked with an asterisk* in the columns headed "In 1801" and "In 1887" respectively) together with those who at the present date (being eighty-eight in all) are *Peers of Ireland alone,* such last-named Peerages being numbered severally in the column headed "A."

Mem.—(1) In this table all Peerages held by the *same* person at the time of the Union are reckoned but as one Peerage, *viz.,* that of the highest grade, the number, so reckoned, then existing being 239.

(2) The names of Peerages which, since the Union, have become *extinct,* or have become *merged* in, or been "*promoted*" to Peerages of higher grade still in existence, are printed *in italics.*

(3) The Barony of Dunboyne, was not acknowledged at the time of the Union, but has, since that date, been established. The Earldom of Mornington, the Viscountcies of Mountgarret, Valentia and of Massereene, and the Baronies of Inchiquin of Farnham, and of Cremorne, now existing as separate Peerages, were, at the time of the Union *merged* in Peerages of a higher grade. The Viscountcies of Clermont, and of O'Neill, and the Baronies of Braudon and of Castlecoote were, also, then so *merged,* but, though they subsequently emerged, are now (1887) *extinct.*

By whom cr.	Date.	DUKES.	Surname.	In 1801.	In 1887.	"A."
Geo. III.	1766	Leinster	Fitz-Gerald	*1	*1	
Victoria	1868	[By "Promotion" since the Union] Abercorn (see Viscountcy of Strabane, *cr.* 1701)	Hamilton	...	*2	
		Total number of DUKES ...		1	2	...

By whom cr.	Date.	MARQUESSES.	Surname.	In 1801.	In 1887.	"A."
Geo. III.	1789	Waterford	Beresford	*1	*1	
„	„	Downshire	Hill	*2	*2	
„	1791	Donegal	Chichester	*3	*3	
„	„	Drogheda	Moore	4	*4	
„	1799	*Wellesley; ex.* 1842, the Earldom of Mornington, *cr.* 1760, remaining	Wellesley	*5	*ex.*	
„	1800	*Thomond ; ex.* 1855, the Barony of Inchiquin, *cr.* 1543, remaining.	O'Brien	6	*ex.*	
„	„	Headfort	Taylour	7	*5	
„	„	Sligo	Browne	8	*6	
„	„	Ely	Loftus	9	*7	

By whom cr.	Date.	MARQUESSES.	Surname.	In 1801.	In 1887	"A.
		[By "Promotion" since the Union]				
Geo. III.	1816	Ormonde ; e.c. 1820 (see Earldoms of Ossory and Ormonde, cr. 1528 and 1541)	Butler	...	ex.	
„	1816	Londonderry (see Earldom of Londonderry, cr. 1796)	Stewart	...	*8	
„	„	Conyngham (see Earldom of Conyngham, cr. 1797)	Conyngham	...	*9	
Geo. IV.	1822	Westmeath; ex. 1871 (see Earldom of Westmeath, cr. 1621)	Nugent	...	ex.	
„	1825	Ormonde (see Earldoms of Ossory and Ormonde, cr. 1528 and 1541)	Butler	...	*10	
„	„	Clanricarde (see Earldom of Clanricarde, cr. 1543)	de Burgh	...	*11	
		Total number of MARQUESSES...		9	11	...

By whom cr.	Date.	EARLS.	Surname.	In 1801.	In 1887	"A."
Hen. VI.	1447	Waterford (Earls of Shrewsbury [E.] having been so cr. in 1442)	Talbot	*1	*1	
Hen. VIII	1528 and 1541	Ossory and Ormonde; pr. 1816 to the Marquessate of Ormonde which became ex. 1820 „ (again) pr. 1825 to the Marquessate of Ormonde	Butler	2	pr.	
„	1543	Clanricarde ; pr. 1825 to the Marquessate of Clanricarde	de Burgh	3	pr.	
James I.	1620	Cork	Boyle	*4	*2	
„	1621	Westmeath; pr. 1822 to the Marquessate of Westmeath which became ex. 1871	Nugent	5	3	1
„	1622	Roscommon ; ex. 1850	Dillon	6	ex.	
„	„	Desmond (Earls of Denbigh [E.] since 1675)	Feilding	*7	*4	
Chas. I.	1627	Meath	Brabazon	8	*5	
„	1628	Barrymore ; ex. 1823	Barry	9	ex.	
„	„	Fingall	Plunkett	10	*6	
„	1647	Cavan	Lambart	11	7	2
Chas. II.	1660	Mountrath ; ex. 1802, the Barony of Castlecoote, cr. with a spec. rem. in 1800 (which also became ex. in 1827) remaining	Coote	12	ex.	
„	1684	Granard	Forbes	13	*8	
Will. III.	1691	Athlone ; ex. 1844	de Ginkell	14	ex.	
Geo. I.	1716	Fitzwilliam (Earls Fitzwilliam [G. B.] 1846)	Fitzwilliam	*15	*9	
„	1722	Kerry (in 1818 this title became united with the [Irish] Earldom of Shelburne [cr. 1753] as also with the Marquessate of Lansdowne in Great Britain)	Fitz-Maurice	16	*10	
„	1725	Darnley	Bligh	*17	*11	
Geo. II.	1733	Egmont	Perceval	*18	*12	
„	1739	Bessborough	Ponsonby	*19	*13	
„	1748	Carrick	Butler	20	14	3

By whom cr.	Date.	EARLS.	Surname.	In 1801.	In 1887.	"A."
Geo. II.	1751	*Upper Ossory ; cx.* 1818	Fitz-Patrick	*21	*ex.*	
„	1753	*Shelburne ; merg.* 1818 in the Earldom of Kerry (Marquesses of Lansdowne [G.B.] 1784)	Fitz-Maurice — Petty	*22	*merg.*	
„	1756	Shannon	Boyle	*23	*15	
' '	„	*Massereene ; cx.* 1816 ; the Viscountcy of Massereene, *cr.* 1660, remaining	Skeffington	24	*ex.*	
„	„	Lanesborough	Butler	25	16	4
„	„	*Belvidere ; cx.* 1814	Rochfort	26	*cx.*	
„	1759	Fife	Duff	27	*17	
„	1760	Mornington. In 1801, this title was *merg.* in the Marquessate of Wellesley, *cr.* 1799 and *cx.* 1842. It then passed to the 1st Baron Maryborough, [U.K.] and so to his son, the 2nd Lord, on whose death in 1863, it passed to the 2nd Duke of Wellington, [U.K.]	Wellesley	*merg.*	*18	
„	„	*Ludlow ; cx.* 1842	Ludlow	28	*ex.*	
Geo. III.	1761	*Tyrconnel ; cx.* 1853	Carpenter	29	*cx.*	
„	„	*Moira* (afterwards, 1816 to 1868, *Marquesses of Hastings,* [U.K.]), *ex.* 1868	Rawdon, afterwards Rawdon-Hastings	*30	*cx.*	
„	1762	Arran	Gore	31	*19	
„	„	Courtown	Stopford	*32	*20	
„	1763	Milltown	Leeson	33	21	5
„	„	Charlemont	Caulfeild	34	*22	
„	1764	*Connaught (Duke of Gloucester and Edinburgh* [G.B.] in the same patent) ; *cx.* 1834	H.R.H.Prince William-Henry	*35	*cx.*	
„	1766	Mexborough	Savile	36	23	6
„	„	Winterton	Turnour	37	24	7
„	1767	Howth	St. Lawrence	38	*25	
„	1768	Kingston	King	39	26	8
„	1771	Sefton	Molyneux	40	*27	
„	„	Roden	Jocelyn	41	*28	
„	1772	*Ross[1] ; cr.* 1802	Gore	42	*cx.*	
„	1776	Lisburne	Vaughan	43	29	9
„	„	Clanwilliam	Meade	44	*30	
„	„	Nugent (Marquesses of Buckingham [G.B.], 1784 ; afterwards [1822], Dukes of Buckingham and Chandos [U.K.])	Nugent afterwards Grenville	*45	*31	
„	„	*Glandore ; cr.* 1815, the Barony of Brandon *cr.* 1758(which also became *cx.* in 1832) remaining	Crosbie	46	*ex.*	
„	1777	*Aldborough ; cx.* 1875	Stratford	47	*cx.*	
„	„	*Clermont ; ex.* 1806, the Viscountcy of Clermont *cr.* 1776 (which also became *ex.* in 1829) remaining	Fortescue	48	*ex.*	
„	1781	Mountcashell	Moore	49	32	10

[1] This must not be confounded with the Earldom of Rosse, conferred in 1806, "by *promotion*" on (Parsons), Baron (and Viscount) Oxmantown.

By whom cr.	Date.	EARLS.	Surname.	In 1801.	In 1887.	"A."
Geo. III.	1784	Ulster (Duke of York and Albany [G.B.] in the same patent) ex. 1827	H.R.H.Prince Frederick	50*	ex.	
„	1785	Antrim, the then Earl of Antrim being so cr. with a spec. rem. [In 1801 this peerage was held by a female]	McDonnel	51	33	11
„	„	Longford	Pakenham	52	*34	
„	„	Portarlington	Dawson	53	35	12
„	„	Farnham ; ex. 1822, the Barony of Farnham, cr. 1756, remaining	Maxwell	54	ex.	
„	„	Carhampton ; ex. 1829	Luttrell	55	ex.	
„	„	Mayo	Bourke	56	36	13
	1789	Munster (cr. Duke of Clarence and St. Andrew's [G.B.] in the same patent) mcry. in the Crown, 1830	H.R.H.Prince William-Henry	57*	ex.	
„	„	Annesley	Annesley	58	37	14
„	„	Enniskillen	Cole	59	*38	
„	„	Erne	Creighton	60	*39	
„	„	Carysfort	Proby	61	*40	
	1793	Kilkenny ; ex. 1846, the Viscountey of Mountgarret, cr. 1550, remaining	Butler	62	ex.	
„	„	Mountnorris ; ex. 1844, the Viscountey of Valentia, cr. 1621, remaining	Annesley	63	ex.	
„	„	Desart	Cuffe	64	41	15
„	„	Wicklow [In 1801, this peerage was held by a female]	Howard	65	42	16
„	„	Clonmell	Scott	66	43	17
„	„	Macartney ; ex. 1806	Macartney	*67	ex.	
„	1795	Clare ; ex. 1864	Fitz Gibbon	*68	ex.	
„	„	Leitrim	Clements	69	*44	
„	„	Lucan	Bingham	70	45	18
„	1796	Londonderry ; pr. 1816, to the Marquessate of Londonderry	Stewart	71	pr.	
„	1797	Belmore	Corry	72	46	19
„	„	Conyngham ; pr. 1816, to the Marquessate of Conyngham	Conyngham	73	pr.	
„	„	Llandaff ; ex. 1833	Mathew	74	ex.	
„	1799	Dublin (Duke of Kent and Edinburgh [G.B.] in the same patent) ; ex. 1820	H.R.H.Prince Edward	75*	ex.	
„	„	Armagh (Duke of Cumberland and Tiviotdale [G.B.] in the same patent). The grantee became King of Hanover, 20 June, 1837[1]	H.R.H.Prince Ernest-Augustus	76*	*47	
„	1800	O'Neill ; ex. 1841, the Viscountey of O'Neill, cr. 1795 (which also became ex. in 1855), remaining	O'Neill	77	ex.	

[1] The two younger sons of George III received titles taken *from* Ireland, but their respective Peerages being created *after* the Union were not Irish Peerages but Peerages of the U.K. The Barony of *Arklow* was conferred with the Dukedom of Sussex, and the Earldom of *Tipperary* with the Dukedom of Cambridge, both on 27 Nov.1801.

By whom cr.	Date.	EARLS.	Surname.	In 1801.	In 1887.	"A."
Geo. III.	1800	Bandon	Bernard	78	48	20
,,	,,	Castle Stewart	Stewart	79	49	21
,,	,,	Donoughmore	Hely-Hutchinson	80	*50	
,,	,,	Caledon	Alexander	81	51	22
,,	,,	Kenmare[1]	Browne	82	*52	
		[By "Promotion" since the Union.]				
,,	1803	Limerick (see Viscountcy of Limerick, cr. 1800)	Pery	...	*53	
,,	,,	Clancarty (see Viscountcy of Dunlo, cr. 1800)	Trench	...	*54	
,,	1806	Gosford (see Viscountcy of Gosford, cr. 1785)	Acheson	...	*55	
,,	,,	*Blessington;* ex. 1829 (see Viscountcy of Mountjoy, cr. 1795, ex. 1829)	Gardiner	...	ex.	
,,	,,	Rosse (see Barony of Oxmantown, cr. 1792)	Parsons	...	56	23
,,	,,	Normanton (see Viscountcy of Somerton, cr. 1800)	Agar	...	*57	
,,	,,	*Charleville;* ex. 1875 (see Viscountcy of Charleville, cr. 1800; ex. 1875)	Bury	...	ex.	
,,	1816	Bantry (see Viscountcy of Bantry, cr. 1800	White	...	58	24
,,	,,	*Glengall;* ex. 1858 (see Barony of Cahir, cr. 1585; ex. 1858)	Butler	...	ex.	
,,	,,	Sheffield (see Barony of Sheffield, cr. 1781)	Holroyd	...	*59	
Geo. IV.	1822	Kilmorey (see Viscountcy of Kilmorey, cr. 1625)	Needham	...	60	25
,,	,,	*Rathdown;* ex. 1848 (see Viscountcy of Monck, cr 1800)	Monck	...	ex.	
,,	,,	Listowel (see Barony of Ennismore, cr. 1800)	Hare	...	*61	
,,	,,	Dunraven (see Barony of Adare, cr. 1800)	Quin	..	*62	
		[By Creation, since the Union.]	Toler	..	63	26
,,	1827	Norbury				
		[By "Promotion" since the Union.]				
Will. IV.	1831	Ranfurly (see Viscountcy of Northland, cr. 1791)	Knox	..	*64	
		Total number of EARLDOMS ..		82	64	26

[1] The last Earldom conferred before the Union was that of *Clanricarde,* the then Earl of Clanricarde being so cr. with special remainder. This Earldom continues (1887), as in 1801, *merged* in the ancient Earldom of 1543, which, in 1825, was *pr.* to a Marquessate.

By whom cr.	Date.	VISCOUNTS.	Surname.	In 1801.	In 1887.	"A."
Ed. IV.	1478	Gormanston (recognised by writ of summons, 2 Aug. 1800)	Preston	1	*1	
Ed. VI,	1550	**Mountgarret** (In 1801, this title was *merg.* in the *Earldom of Kilkenny, cr.* 1793 ; *ex.* 1846)	Butler	*merg.*	2	1
James I.	1621	Grandison (Earls of Jersey [E.], since 1766)	Villiers	*2	*3	
,,	,,	**Valentia** (In 1801, this title was *merg.* in the *Earldom of Mountnorris, cr.* 1792 ; *ex.* 1844)	Annesley	*merg.*	4	2
,,	,,	Dillon	Dillon	3	5	3
,,	1622	*Netterville ; ex.* 1882	Netterville	4	*ex.*	
Chas. I.	1625	*Kilmorey ; pr.* 1822 to the Earldom of Kilmorey	Needham	5	*pr.*	
,,	1628	Lumley (Viscounts Lumley [E.], 1689, Earls of Scarbrough [E.], 1690)	Lumley	*6 / 7	*6 / *ex.*	
,,	,,	*Strangford ; ex.* 1869	Smythe			
,,	,,	Taaffe	Taaffe	8	7	4
,,	,,	*Ranelagh ; ex.* 1885	Jones	9	*ex.*	
,,	1629	*Fitzwilliam ; ex.* 1833[1]	Fitzwilliam	10	*ex.*	
,,	1642	*Cullen ; ex.* 1810[2]	Cokayne	11	*ex.*	
,,	1643	*Bulkeley ; ex.* 1822	Bulkeley	*12	*ex.*	
,,	1646	*Barnewell of Kingsland,* or *Kingsland ; ex.* 1833	Barnewall	13	*ex.*	
Chas. II.	1660	**Massereene** (In 1801, this title was *merg.* in the *Earldom of Massereene, cr.* 1756; *ex.* 1816. In 1843 it became united with the (Irish) Viscountcy of Ferrard)	Skeffington	*merg.*	*8	
,,	1661	Cholmondeley of Kells (Earls Cholmondeley [E.], 1706, and afterwards [1815] Marquesses Cholmondeley [U.K.])	Cholmondeley	*14	*9	
,,	1680	Downe [The Barony in Great Britain held herewith in 1801, became *extinct* in 1832]	Dawney	*15	10	5
Will. III.	1701	*Howe ; ex.* 1814	Howe	16	*c.r.*	
,,	,,	*Strabane* (Earls of Abercorn in Scotland, 1606 ; Marquesses of Abercorn [G.B.], 1790) ; *pr.* 1868, to the Dukedom of Abercorn	Hamilton	*17	*pr.*	
Geo. I.	1716	Molesworth	Molesworth	18	11	6

[1] The Viscountcy of Fitzwilliam *of Merrion,* conferred, 1629, on a family settled in Ireland since the time of Edward II, must not be confounded with the Barony of Fitzwilliam, conferred 1620, and the Earldom, conferred 1716, on the *English* family of Fitzwilliam, both of which last honours are vested in the present (1887) Earl Fitzwilliam in the Peerage of Great Britain.

[2] The heirs male of the body of the first Viscount having failed in 1810, the title was considered as having become *extinct* and was accordingly used as one of the three extinctions required for the creation of the Barony of Howden, in 1819. According, however, to the docquet (the patent being lost and never having been enrolled) this Peerage should have devolved, under a *special remainder,* to the then Earl of Lindsey, a descendant of Martha, Dowager Countess of Holderness (by Montagu Bertie, Lord Willoughby of Eresby, afterwards 2d Earl of Lindsey) sister of Charles Cokayne, the 1st Viscount Cullen. The present (1887) Earl would, according to this docquet, be entitled to this dignity.

By whom cr.	Date.	VISCOUNTS.	Surname.	In 1801.	In 1887.	"A."
Geo I.	1717	Chetwynd	Chetwynd	19	12	7
,,	,,	Midleton	Brodrick	20	*13	
,,	,,	Boyne	Hamilton	21	*14	
,,	,,	Allen ; ex. 1846	Allen	22	ex.	
,,	1719	Grimston (afterwards, 1815, Earl of Verulam [U.K.]	Grimston	*23	*15	
,,	1720	Barrington	Barrington	24	*16	
,,	,,	Gage	Gage	*25	*17	
,,	1722	Palmerston ; cr. 1865	Temple	26	ex.	
,,	1725	Bateman ; ex. 1802	Bateman	27	ex.	
Geo. II.	1727	Galway	Monckton	28	*18	
,,	1743	Powercourt	Wingfield	29	*19	
,,	1751	Ashbrook	Flower	30	20	8
Geo. III.	1763	Mountmorres	Morres, afterwards Montmorency	31	21	9
,,	1766	Dungannon ; ex. 1862	Hill-Trevor	32	ex.	
,,	1776	Southwell	Southwell	33	22	10
,,	,,	De Vesci	Vesey	34	*23	
,,	',,	[Clermont; emerged, 1806, from the Earldom of Clermont (cr. 1777 ; ex. 1806) ; ex. 1829]	Fortescue	merg.	ex.	
,,	1781	Lifford	Hewitt	35	24	11
,,	,,	Bangor	Ward	36	25	12
,,	,,	Melbourne ; ex. 1853	Lamb	37	ex.	
,,	,,	Clifden[1]	Agar	38	*26	
,,	1785	Cremorne ; ex. 1813, the Barony of Cremorne, cr. 1797, remaining	Dawson	39	ex.	
,,	,,	Gosford ; pr. 1806, to the Earldom of Gosford	Acheson	40	pr.	
,,	,,	{ Wicklow ; merg. 1807, in the Earldom of Wicklow, cr. 1793 }	Howard	41	merg.	
,,	,,	Doneraile	St. Leger	42	27	13
,,	,,	Pery ; ex. 1806	Pery	43	ex.	
,,	1791	Northland ; pr. 1831, to the Earldom of Ranfurly	Knox	44	pr.	
,,	,,	Harberton	Pomeroy	45	28	14
,,	1793	Hawarden (afterwards, 1886, Earl de Montalt [U.K.]	Maude	46	*29	
,,	1795	Mountjoy ; pr. 1806, to the Earldom of Blessington. Both peerages ex 1829	Gardiner	47	ex.	
,,	,,	Oxmantown ; ex. 1807 (the Barony of Oxmantown, cr. 1793, and the Earldom of Rosse [a " promotion " of the said Barony], cr. 1806 remaining)	Parsons	48	ex.	
,,	,,	[O'Neill ; emerged, 1841, from the Earldom of O'Neill (cr. 1800 ; ex. 1841) ; ex. 1855]	O'Neill	merg.	ex.	
,,	1797	Carleton ; ex. 1826	Carleton	49	ex.	
,,	,,	Ferrard ; (In 1801, this peerage was held by a female). Merg. 1843, in the Viscountcy of Massereene, cr. 1660	Foster	50	merg.	

[1] The Barony of Mendip [U.K.], by which Viscount Clifden is entitled to an hereditary seat in the House of Lords, was not acquired by a direct creation, but was inherited 2 Feby., 1802, under a special limitation in the patent of the creation thereof in 1794.

By whom cr.	Date.	VISCOUNTS.	Surname.	In 1801.	In 1887.	"A."
Geo. III.	1800	*Limerick ;* pr. 1803, to the Earldom of Limerick	Pery	51	*pr.*	
„	„	*Somerton ;* pr. 1806, to the Earldom of Normanton	Agar	52	*pr.*	
„	„	Avonmore	Yelverton	53	30	15
„	„	*Longueville ; ex.* 1811	Longfield	54	*ex.*	
„	„	*Bantry :* pr. 1816, to the Earldom of Bantry	White	55	*pr.*	
„	„	Monck ; pr. 1822, to the *Earldom of Rathdown,* which Earldom, became *ex.* in 1848	Monck	56	*31	
„	„	*Dunlo ;* pr. 1803, to the Earldom of Clancarty	Trench	57	*pr.*	
„	„	*Charleville ;* pr. 1806, to the Earldom of *Charleville.* Both peerages *ex.* 1875	Bury	58	*ex.*	
„	„	*Kilwarden ; ex.* 1800	Wolfe	59	*ex.*	
		[By " Promotion" since the Union.]				
„	1802	*Newcomen : ex.* 1825 (see Barony of Newcomen, cr. 1800 ; *ex.* 1825)	Newcomen	...	*ex.*	
„	1806	Templetown (see Barony of Templetown, cr. 1776)	Upton	...	32	16
„	„	Lismore (see Barony of Lismore, cr. 1785)	O'Callaghan	..	*33	
„	„	*Lorton* (see Barony of Erris, cr. 1800). *Merg.* 1869, in the Earldom of Kingston	King	...	*merg.*	
„	1815	Frankfort de Montmorency (see Barony of Frankfort, cr. 1800)	Morres, *afterwards* Montmorency	...	34	17
„	1816	Gort (see Barony of Kiltarton, cr. 1810)	Vereker, *formerly* Smyth.	..	35	18
Geo. IV.	1822	*Castlemaine ; ex.* 1839 (see Barony of Castlemaine, cr. 1812)	Handcock	...	*ex.*	
		[By Creation, since the Union.]				
Will. IV.	1831	Guillamore	O'Grady	...	36	19
		Total number of VISCOUNTS ..		59	36	19

By whom cr.	Date.	BARONS.	Surname.	In 1801.	In 1887.	"A."
Hen. III.	1223	Kingsale	De Courcy	1	1	1
Edw. IV.	1461	*Trimlestown, dormant* since 1879	Barnewall	2	*dorm.*	
„	„	Dunsany	Plunkett	3	2	2
Hen.VIII	1541	**Dunboyne** (not recognised in 1801)[1]	Butler	...	3	3
„	„	Louth	Plunkett	4	4	4
„	1543	**Inchiquin** (In 1801, this title was *merged* in the *Marquessate of Thomond,* cr. 1800 ; *ex.* 1855)	O'Brien	*merg.*	5	5

[1] This Peerage which had long been dormant, was recognised in 1827, by a decision of the King's Bench of Ireland, and subsequently, 10 Aug. 1860, by the House of Lords,

By whom cr.	Date.	BARONS.	Surname.	In 1801.	In 1887.	"A."
Eliz.	1585	Caher ; pr., 1816, to the Earldom of Glengall. Both peerages c.c. 1858.	Butler	5	c.c.	
James I.	1620	Digby (Barons Digby [G.B.], 1765 ; Earls Digby, [G.B.] 1790-1856)	Digby	*6	*6	
„	„	Blayney ; c.c. 1874	Blayney	7	cx.	
Chas. I.	1626	Sherard (Earls of Harborough [G.B.], 1719-1859)	Sherard	*8	7	6
Anne	1712	Conway (Barons Conway [E.]`\ having been so cr. in 1703 ; Earls of Hertford [G.B.], 1750 ; Marquesses of Hertford [G.B.], 1793	Seymour-Conway	*9	*8	
Geo I.	1715	Carbery	Evans	10	9	7
„	1718	Aylmer	Aylmer	11	10	8
Geo. II.	1753	Milton (Barons Milton [G.B.], 1762-1808 ; Earls of Dorchester [G.B.], 1792-1808), c.c. 1808	Damer	*12	c.c.	
„	1756	**Farnham** (In 1801, this title was merg. in the Earldom of Farnham cr. 1785 and c.c. 1823.	Maxwell	merg.	11	9
„	1758	[Brandon ; emerged, 1801, from the Earldom of Glandore (cr. 1776 and ex. 1815) c.c. 1832]	Crosbie	merg.	cx.	
„	„	Lisle	Lysaght	13	12	10
Geo. III.	1762	Coleraine ; c.c. 1824	Hanger	14	c.c.	
„	„	Clive (Barons Clive [G.B.], 1794. Afterwards (1804) Earls of Powis [U K.])	Clive, afterwards Herbert	*15	*13	
„	1767	Mulgrave (Afterwards, 1812, Earls of Mulgrave [U.K.], and subsequently, 1838, Marquesses of Normanby [U.K.]	Phipps	*16	*14	
„	1770	Arden ; merg. in 1841 in the Earldom of Egmont.	Perceval	17	merg.	
„	1776	Milford; cx. 1823(a)	Philipps	18	cx.	
„	„	Newborough	Wynn	19	15	11
„	„	Macdonald	Macdonald	20	16	12
„	„	Kensington	Edwards	21	*17	
„	„	Westcote (Lords Lyttelton, Barons of Frankley [G.B.] 1794)	Lyttelton	*22	*18	
„	„	Ongley ; c.c. 1877.	Ongley	23	cx.	
„	„	Templetown ; pr. 1806 to the Viscountcy of Templetown	Upton	24	pr.	
„	„	Massey	Massey	25	19	13
„	1777	Rokeby ; cx. 1883.	Robinson	26	c.c.	
„	1781	Muskerry	Deane	27	20	14
„	„	Sheffield ; pr. 1816 to the Earldom of Sheffield	Holroyd	28	pr.	
„	1782	Hood (Viscounts Hood [G.B.] 1796)	Hood	*29	*21	
„	1783	Riversdale ; ex. 1861	Tonson	30	c.c.	

(*) Richard Bulkeley-Philipps Grant, as inheriting the estate of Lord Milford, took the surname of Phillips and was on 21 Sep. 1847 cr. Baron Milford [U.K.] which peerage became cx. on his death without issue 3 Jan. 1857.

By whom cr.	Date.	BARONS.	Surname.	In 1801.	In 1887.	"A."
Geo. III.	1783	Delaval (Baron Delaval [G.B.] 1786-1808), ex. 1808	Delaval	*31	ex.	
,,	,,	Muncaster	Pennington	32	22	15
,,	,,	Penrhyn ; ex. 1808(ᵃ)	Pennant	33	c.x.	
,,	1785	Lismore ; pr. 1806 to the Viscountcy of Lismore	O'Callaghan	34	pr.	
,,	,,	Sunderlin ; ex. 1816	Malone	35	ex.	
,,	1789	Auckland (Baron Auckland [G.B.] 1793)	Eden	*36	*23	
,,	,,	Kilmaine	Browne	37	24	16
,,	,,	Cloncurry	Lawless	38	*25	
,,	,,	Eardley ; ex. 1824	Eardley	39	ex.	
,,	1790	Callan ; ex. 1815	Agar	40	ex.	
,,	,,	Clonbrook	Dillon	41	26	17
,,	1791	St. Helens ; ex. 1839	FitzHerbert	42	c.c.	
,,	1792	Fermanagh (In 1801 this Peerage was held by a Female), ex. 1810	Verney	43	ex.	
,,	,,	Waterpark (In 1801 this Peerage was held by a Female)	Cavendish	44	27	18
,,	,,	Oxmantown; (In 1801 this title was merged in the Viscountcy of Oxmantown, (er. 1795 and ex. 1807), pr. 1806, to the Earldom of Rosse.	Parsons	merg.	pr.	
,,	1794	Graves	Graves	45	28	19
,,	,,	Bridport ; (Viscount Bridport [G.B.] 1800-1814 ; and subsequently, 1868, Viscounts Bridport [U.K.]	Hood	*46	*29	
,,	1795	Kilwarden of Kilteel ; (In 1801, this peerage was held by a female) merg. 1804, in the Viscountcy of Kilwarden. Both Peerages ex. 1830	Wolfe	47	ex.	
,,	,,	Lavington ; ex. 1807	Payne	48	ex.	
,,	,,	Rancliffe ; 1850	Parkyns	49	ex.	
,,	1796	Huntingfield	Vanneck	50	30	20
,,	,,	Carrington (Barons Carrington [G.B.] 1797)	Smith, afterwards Carington	*51	*31	
,,	,,	Rossmore	Cuninghame afterwards Westenra	}52	*32	
,,	1797	Keith ; (Baron Keith [U.K.], 1801 and 1803 ; afterwards, 1814-1828, Viscount Keith [U.K.]) ex. 1867	Elphinstone	53	c.r.	
,,	,,	Hotham	Hotham	54	33	21
,,	,,	Cremorne ; (In 1801, this title was merged in the Viscountcy of Cremorne, er. 1785 and ex. 1813) afterwards, 1866, Earls of Dartrey [U.K.]	Dawson	merg.	*34	
,,	,,	Tyrawly ; er. 1821	Cuffe	55	ex.	

(ᵃ) A Barony of Penrhyn [U.K.] was conferred 3 Aug. 1866 on the Hon. Edward Gordon Douglas-Pennant, who had married the eldest daughter of George Hay Dawkins-Pennant of Penrhyn Castle, the cousin and heir of Lord Penrhyn in the Peerage of Ireland (abovenamed) who died in 1808.

By whom cr.	Date.	BARONS.	Surname.	In 1801.	In 1887.	"A."
Geo. III.	1797	Norwood; (In 1801, this peerage was held by a female) merg., 1832, in the Earldom of Norbury	Toler	56	merg.	
,,	,,	Headley	Allanson-Winn	57	35	22
,,	,,	Teignmouth	Shore	58	36	23
,,	,,	Holmes; cx. 1804	Holmes	59	c.c.	
,,	,,	Crofton (In 1801, this peerage was held by a female)	Crofton	60	37	24
,,	1798	French (In 1801, this peerage was held by a female)	French	61	38	25
,,	1799	Henley	Eden, afterwards Henley	62	*39	
,,	1800	Whitworth; afterwards 1813-1825, Viscount Whitworth [U.K] and subsequently 1815-1825, Earl Whitworth [U.K.] c.c. 1825.	Whitworth	63	c.c.	
,,	,,	[Castlecoote; emerged, 1802, from the Earldom of Mountrath, (cr. 1660 and cx. 1802) e.c. 1827]	Coote	merg.	c.c.	
,,	,,	Langford	Rowley	64	40	26
,,	,,	De Blaquiere	Blaquiere	65	41	27
,,	,,	Frankfort; pr. 1816 to the Vis-county of Frankfort de Mont-morency	Morres, afterwards Mount-morency	66	pr.	
,,	,,	Dufferin; (In 1801, this peerage was held by a female). Subsequently, 1871, Earl of Dufferin [U.K.]	Blackwood	67	*42	
,,	,,	Henniker	Henniker	68	*43	
,,	,,	Newcomen; (In 1801, this peerage was held by a female) pr. 1802, to the Viscountey of Newcomen. Both peerages cx. 1825	Newcomen	69	cx.	
,	,,	Adare; pr. 1822, to the Earldom of Dunraven and Mount Earl	Quin	70	pr.	
,,	,,	Ventry	Mullins	71	44	28
,,	,,	Ennismore; pr. 1822, to the Earldom of Listowel	Hare	72	pr.	
,,	,,	Wallscourt	Blake	73	45	29
,,	,,	Mount Sandford; cx. 1846	Sandford	74	c.r.	
,,	,,	Dunalley	Prittie	75	46	30
,,	,,	Tara; er. 1821	Preston	76	c.c.	
,,	,,	Hartland; cx. 1845	Mahon	77	cx.	
,,	,,	Clanmorris	Bingham	78	47	31
,,	,,	Leeale; cx. 1810	Fitz Gerald	79	c.c.	
,,	,,	Radstock	Waldegrave	80	48	32
,,	,,	Glenbervie; cx. 1823	Douglas	81	c.c.	
,,	,,	Norbury; merg. 1831, in the Barony of Norwood (er. 1797), both Baronies becoming, subsequently, 1832, merg., in the Earldom of Norbury	Toler	82	merg.	
,,	,,	Gardner,[a]	Gardner	83	*49	

(a) Since 2 Nov. 1883, the right to this Peerage is dormant. It is, however, unquestionably, not extinct, though omitted by Sir Bernard Burke, in his "Ulsters Roll" of 1887.

By whom cr.	Date.	BARONS.	Surname.	In 1801.	In 1887	"A."
Geo. III.	1800	Nugent; (In 1801, this peerage was held by a female, the Marchioness of Buckingham, on whom it had been conferred for life) c.c. 1812	Temple-Nugent Grenville	84	c.c.	
"	"	Nugent; c.c. 1850	"	85	c.c.	
"	"	Ashtown	Trench	86	50	33
"	"	Clarina	Massey	87	51	34
"	"	Erris ; pr. 1806, to the Viscountcy of Lorton, both peerages becoming, subsequently, 1869, mery. in the Earldom of Kingston	King	88	pr. and mery.	
		[By Creation since the Union.]				
"	1806	Rendlesham	Thellusson	...	52	35
"	1810	Kiltarton ; pr. 1816, to the Viscountcy of Gort	Smyth, (afterwards Vereker)	...	pr.	
"	1812	Castlemaine ; pr. 1822, to the Viscountcy of Castlemaine, which last became c.c. 1839	Handcock	...	53	36
"	"	Decies	Beresford	...	54	37
"	1818	Garvagh	Canning	...	55	38
"	1819	Howden; c.c. 1873	Cradock	...	cr.	
Geo. IV.	1822	Downes ; c.c. 1863	Downes	...	c.c.	
"	1825	Bloomfield ; cr. 1879	Bloomfield	...	c.c.	
"	1826	Fitz Gerald and Vesey ; cr. 1860	Vesey-Fitz-Gerald	...	cx.	
Will. IV.	1831	Talbot of Malahide	Talbot	...	*56	
"	1834	Carew	Carew	...	*57	
"	1836	Oranmore and Browne	Browne	...	58	39
Victoria	1845	Dunsandle and Clanconal	Daly	..	59	40
"	1848	Bellew	Bellew	...	60	41
"	1852	Clermont	Fortescue	...	*61	
"	1856	Fermoy	Roche	...	62	42
"	1863	Athlumney	Somerville	...	*63	
"	1868	Rathdonnell	McClintock	...	64	43
		Total number of BARONIES ...		88	64	43

SUMMARY OF TABLE I.

	In 1801.	In 1887.	"A."
DUKES · · · · · ·	1	2	...
MARQUESSES · · · · · ·	9	11	...
EARLS · · · · · · ·	82	64	26
VISCOUNTS · · · · · ·	59	36	19
BARONS (excluding, in 1801, the Barony of Dunboyne, the right to which was not then acknowledged, but including the same in 1887) · · · ·	88	64	43
TOTAL ·	239	(^)177	88

(^) In 1887, out of this number of 177, the 2 Dukes ; the 11 Marquesses ; 38, out of the 64, Earls ; 17, out of the 36, Viscounts: and 21, out of the 64, Barons (viz.: 89 Peers in all) possessed an hereditary peerage in the House of Lords, leaving 88 *Peers possessing Peerages of Ireland alone* as in column "A."

TABLE II.

Peerages *existing* at the time of the Union (1 Jany. 1801) of which the creation was anterior to the accession of George III (the then reigning Monarch), arranged chronologically, according the date of the *most ancient peerage* enjoyed by the then Peer.

ELEVEN CREATIONS PRIOR TO (1485) THE ACCESSION OF THE HOUSE OF TUDOR.

11 **Earldoms**, *viz.* (1) KILDARE (*Fitz Gerald*), 1316, Marquesses of Kildare since 1761, Dukes of Leinster since 1766; (2) WATERFORD (*Talbot*), 1447, Earls of Shrewsbury in England. 11 **Viscountcies**, *viz.* (1) BUTTEVANT (*Barry*), 1461? Earls of Barrymore, 1628 to 1823, *extinct* 1823; (2) GORMANSTON (*Preston*). VII **Baronies**, *viz.* (1) KINGSALE (*De Courcy*), 1223?; (2) KERRY (*Fitzmaurice*), Earls of Kerry since 1722, also, since 1818, Marquesses of Lansdowne in the U.K. and Earls of Shelburne; (3) DELVIN (*Nugent*), Earls of Westmeath since 1621, Marquesses, 1822 to 1871; (4) KILLEEN (*Plunkett*), Earls of Fingall since 1628; (5) HOWTH (*St. Lawrence*), Earls of Howth, since 1767; (6) TRIMLESTON (*Barnewall*), 1461, *extinct* or *dormant*, 1879; (7) DUNSANY (*Plunkett*), 1461? To which, may possibly be added the anomalous Barony of LA POER, if its date can be considered as being that of a Barony of (*Power*) 1375, instead of a Barony of (*Beresford*) 1767.

SEVEN CREATIONS BY THE HOUSE OF TUDOR, 1485 to 1603.

11 **Earldoms**, *viz.* (1) OSSORY and ORMONDE (*Butler*), 1528 and 1541, Marquesses of Ormonde 1816 to 1820 and (again) since 1825; (2) CLANRICARDE (*De Burgh*), 1543, Marquesses of Clanricarde since 1825. 1 **Viscountcy**, *viz.* MOUNTGARRET (*Butler*), 1550; Earls of Kilkenny 1793 to 1846. IV **Baronies**, *viz.* (1) DUNBOYNE(ᵃ) (*Butler*), 1550; (2) LOUTH (*Plunkett*), 1541; (3) INCHIQUIN (*O'Brien*), 1543, Earls of Inchiquin 1654 to 1855, Marquesses of Thomond 1800 to 1855; (4) CAHER (*Butler*), 1582, Earls of Glengall, 1816 to 1858, *extinct* 1858.

THIRTY-EIGHT CREATIONS (*de novo*) BY THE HOUSES OF STUART AND NASSAU, 1603 to 1714, *exclusive* of Peerages of higher grade conferred on existing Peers.—

111 **Earldoms**, *viz.* (1) DESMOND (*Feilding*), 1622, Earls of Denbigh in England since 1675; (2) MOUNTRATH (*Coote*), 1660, *extinct* 1802; (3) ATHLONE (*De Ginkell*) 1691, *extinct* 1844. XXIII **Viscountcies**, *viz.* (1) GRANDISON (*St. John*, afterwards *Villiers*), 1621, Earls of Jersey in England since 1766; (2) VALENTIA (*Annesley*), 1621, Earls Mountnorris 1793 to 1844; (3) DILLON (*Dillon*), 1621; (4) NETTERVILLE (*Netterville*), 1622, *extinct* 1882; (5) CHICHESTER (*Chichester*), 1625, Earls of Donegall since 1647, Marquesses since 1791; (6) KILMOREY (*Needham*), 1625, Earls of Kilmorey since 1822; (7) LUMLEY (*Lumley*), 1628, Earls of Scarbrough in England since 1689; (8) STRANGFORD (*Smythe*), 1628, *extinct* 1869; (9) TAAFFE (*Taaffe*), 1628; (10) RANELAGH (*Jones*), 1628, *extinct* 1885; (11) MOLYNEUX (*Molyneux*), 1628, Earls of Sefton since 1771; (12) IKERRIN (*Butler*), 1629, Earls of Carrick since 1740; (13) FITZWILLIAM OF MERRION (*Fitzwilliam*), 1629, *extinct* 1833; (14) CULLEN (*Cokayne*), 1642, *extinct* 1810; (15) BULKELEY (*Bulkeley*), 1643, *extinct* 1822; (16) BARNEWALL OF KINGSLAND (*Barnewall*), 1646, *extinct* 1833; (17) MASSEREENE (*Skeffington*), 1660, Earls of Massereene 1756 to 1816; (18) CHOLMONDELEY (*Cholmondeley*), 1661, Earls Cholmondeley in England since 1706, Marquesses in the U.K. since 1815; (19) GRANARD (*Forbes*), 1675, Earls of Granard since 1684; (20) DOWNE (*Dawney*) 1680; (21) LISBURNE (*Vaughan*), Earls of Lisburne since 1776; (22) HOWE (*Howe*), 1701, *extinct* 1814; (23) STRABANE (*Hamilton*) 1701, Earls of Abercorn in Scotland, also, since 1790, Marquesses of Abercorn in Great Britain, and, since 1868, Dukes of Abercorn. XII **Baronies**, *viz.* (1) BRABAZON (*Brabazon*) 1626, Earls of Meath since 1627; (2) MOORE (*Moore*) 1616, Viscounts Moore of Drogheda since 1621, Earls of Drogheda since 1661, Marquesses since 1791; (3) BOYLE (*Boyle*) 1616, Earls of Cork since 1620; (4) LAMBART (*Lambart*) 1617, Earls of Cavan since 1647; (5) KILKENNY WEST (*Dillon*) 1629, Earls of Roscommon, 1622 to 1850, *extinct* 1850; (6) CASTLE STEWART (*Stewart*) 1619, Earls Castle Stewart since 1800; (7) DIGBY (*Digby*) 1620, Earls Digby in Great Britain, 1790 to 1856; (8) FITZWILLIAM (*Fitzwilliam*) 1620, Earls Fitzwilliam since 1726 also Earls Fitzwilliam in G.B. since 1746; (9) CAULFEILD (*Caulfeild*) 1620, Viscounts Charlemont since 1665, Earls since 1763; (10) BLAYNEY (*Blayney*) 1621, *extinct* 1874; (11) SHERARD (*Sherard*) 1626, Earls of Harborough in G.B. 1719 to 1859; (12) CONWAY (*Seymour-Conway*) 1712, Barons Conway in England, also, since 1750, Earls and since 1793, Marquesses of Hertford in G.B.

(ᵃ) The Barony of Dunboyne was not recognised as the time of the Union. See, *ante*, p. 16, note 1.

Forty-nine creations (*de novo*) by the House of Hanover, 1714 to 1760 (25 Oct.), the date of the accession of George III, (the reigning Sovereign at the time of the Union *exclusive* of Peerages of higher grade conferred on existing Peers.

1 **Earldom**, *viz.* SHANNON (*Boyle*), 1756.   XIV **Viscountcies**, *viz.* (1) MOLESWORTH (*Molesworth*), 1716 ; (2) CHETWYND (*Chetwynd*, 1717 ; (3) HILLSBOROUGH (*Hill*), 1717, Earls of Hillsborough since 1751 (also Earls of Hillsborough in G.B., since 1772), Marquesses of Downshire since 1789 ; (4) ALLEN (*Allen*), 1717, *extinct* 1816 ; (5) GRIMSTON (*Grimston*), 1719, Earls of Verulam in the U.K. since 1815 ; (6) BARRINGTON (*Shute-Barrington*), 1720 ; (7) GAGE (*Gage*), 1720 ; (8) TYRONE (*Beresford*), 1720, Earls of Tyrone since 1746, Marquesses of Waterford since 1789 ; (9) PALMERSTON (*Temple*), 1722, *extinct* 1865 ; (10) BATEMAN (*Bateman*), 1725, *extinct* 1802 ; (11) GALWAY (*Monckton*), 1727 ; (12) POWERSCOURT (*Wingfield*), 1743 ; (13) FITZMAURICE (*Fitzmaurice-Petty*), 1751, Earls of Shelburne since 1753 (honours which, in 1818, *merged* into the Earldom of Kerry), Marquesses of Lansdowne in the U.K. since 1784 ; (14) SUDLEY (*Gore*), 1758, Earls of Arran since 1762.   XXXIV **Baronies**, *viz.* (1) BRODRICK (*Brodrick*), 1717, Viscounts Midleton since 1717 ; (2) PERCEVAL (*Perceval*), 1715, Viscounts Perceval since 1722, Earls of Egmont since 1733 ; (3) GOWRAN (*Fitzpatrick*), 1715, Earls of Upper Ossory, 1751 to 1818, *extinct* 1818 ; (4) CARBERY (*Evans*) 1715 ; (5) HAMILTON (*Hamilton*) 1715, Viscounts Boyne since 1717 ; (6) BUTLER (*Butler*), 1715, Viscounts Lanesborough since 1728, Earls of Lanesborough since 1756 ; (7) SOUTHWELL (*Southwell*), 1717, Viscounts Southwell since 1776 ; (8) AYLMER (*Aylmer*), 1718 ; (9) CARPENTER (*Carpenter*) 1719, Earls of Tyrconnel, 1761 to 1853, *extinct* 1853 ; (10) BESSBOROUGH (*Ponsonby*), 1719, Viscounts Duncannon since 1722, Earls of Bessborough since 1739 ; (11) CLIFTON (*Bligh*), 1721, Viscounts Darnley since 1723, Earls since 1725 ; (12) CASTLEDURROW (*Flower*), 1733, Viscounts Ashbrook since 1751 ; (13) DESART (*Cuffe*), 1733, Viscounts Desart since 1781, Earls since 1793 ; (14) BRACO (*Duff*), 1735, Earls Fife, since 1759 ; (15) BELLFIELD (*Rochfort*), 1737, Viscounts Bellfield 1751 to 1814, Earls of Belvidere 1756 to 1814, *extinct* 1814 ; (16) NEWPORT (*Jocelyn*) 1743, Viscounts Jocelyn since 1755, Earls of Roden since 1771 ; (17) MORNINGTON (*Wellesley*), 1746 Earls of Mornington since 1760, Marquess Wellesley 1799 to 1842, Dukes of Wellington in the U.K. since 1863 ; (18) RAWDON (*Rawdon*), 1750, Earls of Moira 1761 to 1868, also Marquesses of Hastings in the U.K. 1815 to 1868, *extinct* 1868 ; (19) KNAPTON (*Vesey*) 1750, Viscounts de Vesey since 1776 ; (20) CARYSFORT (*Proby*), 1751, Earls of Carysfort since 1789 ; (21) MILTON (*Damer*), 1753, Earls of Dorchester in G.B., 1792 to 1808, *extinct* 1808 ; (22) POLLINGTON (*Savile*), 1753, Earls of Mexborough since 1766 ; (23) LUDLOW (*Ludlow*), 1753, Earls Ludlow 1760 to 1842, *extinct* 1842 ; (24) LONGFORD (*Pakenham*), 1756, Earls of Longford since 1794 ; (25) MOUNTMORRES (*Morres*), 1756, Viscounts Mountmorres since 1763 ; (26) FARNHAM (*Maxwell*), 1756, Earls of Farnham 1785 to 1823 ; (27) RUSSBOROUGH (*Leeson*) 1756, Viscounts Russborough since 1760, Earls of Milltown since 1763 ; (28) BRANDON (*Crosbie*), 1758, Viscounts Crosbie 1771 to 1815, Earls of Glandore 1776 to 1815, *extinct* 1832 ; (29) ANNESLEY (*Annesley*), 1758, Viscounts Glerawly since 1766, Earls Annesley since 1789 ; (30) COURTOWN (*Stopford*), 1758, Earls of Courtown since 1762 ; (31) LISLE (*Lysaght*), 1758 ; (32) HEADFORT (*Taylor*), 1760, Earls of Bective, since 1766, Marquesses of Headfort since 1800 ; (33) MOUNTFLORENCE (*Cole*), 1760, Viscounts Enniskillen since 1766, Earls since 1789 ; (34) MOUNTEAGLE (*Browne*), 1760, Viscounts Westport since 1768, Earls of Altamont since 1771, Marquesses of Sligo since 1800.

SUMMARY of the above Table of Peerages, anterior to the reign of George III, existing at the time of the Union.

Creations prior to (1485) the accession of the House of Tudor · · ·		11
„	by the House of Tudor, 1485 to 1603, *exclusive* of the Barony of Dunboyne · · · · · · ·	6
„	by the Houses of Stuart and Nassau, 1603 to 1714 · · ·	38
„	by the House of Hanover, 1714 to (the accession of George III) 1760 ·	49
	Total · (ª)104	

(ª) The Barony of Dunboyne, *cr.* 1541, (which was not allowed till after the Union) is deducted herefrom. See, *ante*, p. 16, note I.

So that the addition to the Peerage, by George III from his accession to the Union, of those whose Peerages were at the date of the Union still *extant*, was   135

Total number of Peers existing at the Union as in Table I.   - (a)239

Supplement to Table II.

It must be remembered that out of the holders of the abovenamed 104 Peerages, (*i.e.* Peerages *cr.* anterior to the reign of George III, and still existing at the time of the Union), no less than 34 had obtained *other* Peerages from George III (in all cases but that of Clanricarde) of a HIGHER GRADE. These were I Dukedom, *viz.* Leinster.   VIII Marquessates, *viz.* (1) Waterford; (2) Downshire; (3) Donegall ; (4) Drogheda : (5) Wellesley* ; (6) Thomond* ; (7) Headfort; (8) Sligo.   XXII Earldoms, *viz.* (1) Tyrconnel* ; (2) Moira* ; (3) Arran ; (4) Courtown ; (5) Milltown ; (6) Charlemont; (7) Mexborough ; (8) Howth ; (9) Sefton ; (10) Roden ; (11) Lisburne ; (12) Glandore*; (13) Longford ; (14) Farnham* ; (15) Annesley ; (16) Enniskillen ; (17) Carysfort ; (18) Kilkenny* ; (19) Mountmorris* ; (20) Desart ; (21) Castle Stewart ; (22) Clanricarde ; also III **Viscountcies**, *viz.* (1) Mountmorris ; (2) Southwell ; (3) De Vesci ; Total 34.   The following peerages in G.B. were conferred by George III on the holders of Irish Peerages created before his accession *exclusive* of any conferred on those 34 who had obtained from him higher Peerages (in Ireland) as given above.   These were I **Marquessate**, *viz.* Abercorn [V. Strabane]. II **Earldoms**, *viz.* (1) Digby*; (2) Dorchester* [B. Damer].   VIII **Baronies**, *viz.* (1) Bulkeley* ; (2) Carleton [E. of Shannon] ; (3) Fife* ; (4) Verulam [V. Grimston] ; (5) Gage ; (6) Upper Ossory* ; (7) Dawnay* [V. Down] and (8) Brodrick [V. Midleton]. Total 11.   This number added to the 34 (Irish) Peerages abovenamed makes 45, which added to the 135 creations by George III makes 180, leaving out of the 239(a) Peers existing at the time of the Union but 59 Peers who had not received a Peerage either in Ireland or G.B. from the then reigning monarch.

* These (so marked) were extinct in 1887.

TABLE III.

Peerages which at the time of the Union (1 Jan. 1801) were held, *suo jure*, by Females, arranged *according to their precedence.*

2 EARLDOMS.

| Antrim | | | *cr.* 1785 | Wicklow | | | *cr.* 1793 |

1 VISCOUNTCY.

| | Ferrard | | | *cr.* 1797 |

10 BARONIES.

Arden			*cr.* 1770	Crofton			*cr.* 1797
Fermanagh			„ 1792	French			„ 1798
Waterpark			„ „	Dufferin			„ 1800
Kilwarden of Kilteel			„ 1795	Newcomen			„ „
Norwood.			„ 1797	Nugent			„ „

Total number 13 ; all of them but Nugent, (which had *no* words of remainder) being creations with rem. of the dignity to the heir male of the body of the Grantee, or (as in the case of Antrim) to such heir of the *daughters* of the grantee.(b)

(a) See *ante*, p. 22, note "a."
(b) *Note.* The only Irish Peerage by patent then (1801) and now (1887) existing, of which the rem. was to heirs *general*, was the Viscountcy of Massereene *cr.* 1660.   The anomalous decision in 1769 whereby the Barony of La Poer was (erroneously) allowed to the heir *general*, was founded on the idea that (as in England) a Barony could be created *by writ* in *Ireland* ; an idea not only contrary to all previous practice but even to common sense, making the writ of a Subject (*i.e.* the Lord Lieut. who frequently, *sponte sua*, issued it) equal to that of the Crown,   See [Lynch's] " Remarks upon the ancient Baronage of Ireland," Dublin, 1829, pp. 15-27.

TABLE IV.

Peerage extinct since the date of the Union (1 Jan. 1801) shewing the extinction of *all* Peerages, held by *the same* Person, of which the patents were *distinct*, arranged chronologically.

[*Note*. On 20 Oct. 1800, only a few weeks before the Union, died Charles (Coote), Earl of Bellomont, 5th Baron Coote of Coloony, when all his Peerage honours became *extinct*].

Date of extinction	Date of creation	Title of Peerage.	Rank of Peerage.	Surname of First Peer.	Number of Extinctions.		
					(b)	(c)	(d)
1802	1725	Bateman	V.(a)	Bateman	1	1	
„	1660	Mountrath (the Barony of Castlecoote remaining)	E.	Coote	+	2	
„	1771	Ross	E.	Gore	2	3	
„	1768	Bellisle	V.	„	...	4	
„	1764	Gore	B.	„	...	5	
1804	1797	Holmes	B.	Holmes	3	6	
1806	1785	Pery	V.	Pery	4	7	
„	1794	Macartney	E.	Macartney	5	8	
„	1792	„	V.	„	...	9	
„	1776	„	B.	„	...	10	
.,	1777	Clermont (the Viscountcy of Clermont remaining)	E.	Fortescue	+	11	
1807	1795	Lavington	B.	Payne	6	12	
„	1795	Oxmantown (the Barony of Oxmantown, as, also, the Earldom of Rosse [a "*promotion*"] remaining)	V.	Parsons	+	13	
1808	1783	Penrhyn	B.	Pennant	7	14	
„	1753	Milton (Earl of Dorchester in Great Britain)	B.	Damer	8	15	
„	1783	Delaval	B.	Delaval	9	16	
1810	1800	Lecale	B.	FitzGerald	10	17	
„	1642	Cullen(e)	V.	Cokayne	11	18	
„	1792	Fermanagh	B.	Verney	12	19	
1811	1800	Longueville	V.	Longfield	13	20	
„	1795	„	B.	„	...	21	
1812	1800	Nugent (life peerage conferred on Mary Elizabeth, Marchioness of Buckingham).	B.	Nugent-Temple-Grenville	14	22	
1813	1785	Cremorne (the Barony of Cremorne remaining)	V.	Dawson	+	23	
„	1770	Dartrey	B.	„	...	24	
1814	1756	Belvidere	E.	Rochfort	15	25	
„	1751	Bellfield	V.	„	...	26	
„	1773	„	B.	„	...	27	
„	1701	Howe	V.	Howe	16	28	
1815	1790	Callan	B.	Agar	17	29	
„	1776	Glandore (the Barony of Brandon remaining)	E.	Crosbie	+	30	
„	1771	Crosbie (ditto)	V.	„	...	31	
1816	1785	Sunderlin of Lake Sunderlin	B.	Malone	18	32	
.,	1797	Sunderlin of Baronstown	B.	„	„	33	

(a) " B " denotes "Barony"; "D" denotes "Dukedom"; "E" denotes "Earldom"; ' M " denotes "Marquessate," and "V" denotes "Viscountcy."

(b) Reckoning all Peerages held by the same person on 1 Jan. 1801 as but *one* peerage.

(c) Reckoning each Peerage held by the same person on 1 Jan. 1801, of which the patent was distinct, as a *separate* Peerage.

(d) Extinction of "*Promotions*" only.

(e) See *ante*, p. 14, note 2.

Date of extinction	Date of creation	Title of Peerage.	Rank of Peerage.	Surname of First Peer.	Number of Extinctions (b)	(c)	(d)
1816	1756	Massereene (the Viscountcy of Massereene remaining)	E.(a)	Skeffington	┼	34	
1818	1751	Upper Ossory	E.	FitzPatrick	18	35	
,,	1715	Gowran	B.	,,	...	36	
1820	1799	Dublin (Duke of Kent in G. B.)	E.	H.R.H.Prince Edward	19	37	
,,	1816	Ormonde [the " promotion " only]	M.	Butler	┼	┼	1
1821	1800	Tara	B.	Preston	20	38	
,,	1797	Tyrawly	B.	Cuffe	21	39	
1822	1643	Bulkeley	V.	Bulkeley	22	40	
1823	1800	Glenbervie	B.	Douglas	23	41	
,,	1776	Milford	B.	Philipps	24	42	
,,	1785	Farnham (the Barony of Farnham remaining)	E.	Maxwell	┼	43	
,,	1628	Barrymore	E.	Barry	25	44	
,,	1461?	Buttevant, Barrymore or Barry	V.	,,	...	45	
1824	1761	Coleraine	B.	Hanger	26	46	
,,	1789	Eardley	B.	Eardley	27	47	
1825	1803	Newcomen [a " promotion "]	V.	Newcomen	┼	—	2
,,	1800	,,	B.	,,	28	48	
,,	1800	Whitworth (Earl Whitworth in the United Kingdom)	B.	Whitworth	29	49	
1826	1797	Carleton	V.	Carleton	30	50	
,,	1789	,,	B.	,,	...	51	
1827	1784	Ulster (Duke of York in Great Britain)	E.	H.R.H.Prince Frederick	31	52	
,,	1800	Castlecoote	B.	Coote	32	53	
1829	1784	Carhampton	E.	Luttrell	33	54	
,,	1789	,,	V.	,,	...	55	
,,	1768	Irnham	B.	,,	...	56	
,,	1816	Blesington [a " promotion "]	E.	Gardiner	┼	┼	3
,,	1797	Mountjoy	V.	,,	34	57	
,,	1789	,,	B.	,,	...	58	
,,	1776	Clermont	V.	Fortescue	35	59	
1830	1789	Munster(e) (Duke of Clarence in Great Britain)	E.	H.R.H.Prince William	36	60	
,,	1800	Kilwarden	V.	Wolfe	37	61	
,,	1798	Kilwarden of Newlands	B.	,,	...	62	
,,	1795	Kilwarden of Kilteel(f)	B.	,,	38(f)	63	
1832	1758	Brandon	B.	Crosbie	39	64	
1833	1629	Fitzwilliam of Merrion	V.	Fitzwilliam	40	65	
,,	1797	Llandaff	E.	Mathew	41	66	
,,	1793	,,	V.	,,	...	67	
,,	1783	,,	B.	,,	...	68	
,,	1646	Barnewall of Kingsland	V.	Barnewall	42	69	
1834	1764	Connaught (Duke of Gloucester in Great Britain)	E.	H.R.H.Prince William Henry	43	70	
1839	1822	Castlemaine [the " promotion " only]	V.	Handcock	┼	┼	4

(a) (b) (c) (d) See notes to commencement of this table.

(e) *Merged* in the Crown on the accession thereto of King William IV.

(f) At the time of the Union this Peerage was held by Anne, *suo jure* Baroness Kilwarden of Kilteel, at whose death, 23 Aug. 1804, it merged in the Viscountcy (conferred on her husband) which last title (with the Barony of 1798) had, 23 July 1803, been, previous to her death, inherited by her eldest son.

Date of extinction	Date of creation	Title of Peerage.	Rank of Peerage.	Surname of First Peer.	Number of Extinctions. (b)	(c)	(d)
1839	1791	St. Helens	B.(ᵃ)	Fitzherbert	44	71	
1841	1800	O'Neill (the Viscountcy of O'Neill remaining)	E.	O'Neill	+	72	
1842	1760	Ludlow	F.	Ludlow	45	73	
„	1755	„	B.	„	...	74	
„	1799	Wellesley (the Earldom of Mornington remaining)	M.	Wellesley	+	75	
1844	1691	Athlone	E.	De Ginkell	46	76	
„	1793	Mountnorris (the Viscountcy of Valentia remaining)	E.	Annesley	+	77	
1845	1800	Hartland	B.	Mahon	47	78	
1846	1792	Kilkenny (the Viscountcy of Mountgarret, remaining)	E.	Butler	+	79	
„	1717	Allen	V	Allen	48	80	
„	1800	Mount Sandford	B.	Sandford	49	81	
1849	1822	Rathdown [the "promotion" only]	E.	Monck	+	+	5
1850	1622	Roscommon	E.	Dillon	50	82	
„	1619	Kilkenny West	B.	„	..	83	
„	1795	Rancliffe	B.	Parkyns	51	84	
„	1800	Nugent	B.	Grenville	52	85	
1853	1761	Tyrconnel	E.	Carpenter	53	86	
„	1719	Carpenter	B.	„	...	87	
„	1780	Melbourne	V.	Lamb	54	88	
„	1770	„	B.	„	...	89	
1855	1795	O Neill	V.	O'Neill	55	90	
„	1793	„	B.	„	...	91	
„	1800	Thomond (the Barony of Inchiquin (remaining)	M.	O'Brien	+	92	
„	1654	Inchiquin (do.)	E.	„	...	93	
1858	1816	Glengall [a "promotion"]	E.	Butler	+	+	6
„	1583	Caher	B.	„	56	94	
1860	1826	FitzGerald and Vesey(ᵉ)	B.	FitzGerald	57	95	
1861	1783	Riversdale	B.	Tonson	58	96	
1862	1765	Dungannon	V.	Hill-Trevor	59	97	
1863	1822	Downes(ᵉ)	B.	Downes	60	98	
1864	1795	Clare	E.	FitzGibbon	61	99	
„	1789	FitzGibbon	B.	„	...	100	
1865	1722	Palmerston	V.	Temple	62	101	
1867	1797	Keith	B.	Keith-Elphinstone	63	102	
1868	1761	Moira (M. of Hastings in the U.K.)	E.	Rawdon	64	103	
„	1750	Rawdon (do.)	B.	„	65	104	
1869	1628	Strangford	V.	Smythe	..	105	
1871	1822	Westmeath [the "promotion" only]	M.	Nugent	+	+	7
1873	1810	Howden(ᵉ)	B.	Cradock	66	106	
1874	1621	Blayney	B.	Blayney	67	107	
1875	1806	Charleville [a "promotion"]	E.	Bury	+	—	8
„	1800	„	V.	„	68	108	
„	1797	Tullamoore	B.	„	...	109	
„	1777	Aldborough	E.	Stratford	70	110	
„	1776	„	V.	„	...	111	
„	1763	Baltinglass	B.	„	...	112	
1877	1776	Ongley	B.	Ongley	71	113	

(ᵃ) (ᵇ) (ᶜ) (ᵈ) See notes to commencement of this table.

(ᵉ) These four Peerages, (FitzGerald, Downes, Howden, and Bloomfield) being creations made since the Union, their extinction did not avail as one of the three extinctions required by that act to enable the creation of a new Peerage.

Date of extinction	Date of creation	Title of Peerage.	Rank of Peerage.	Surname of First Peer.	Number of Extinctions.		
					(b)	(c)	(d)
1879	1461	Trimleston(e)	B.(a)	Barnewall	72	114	
..	1825	Bloomfield(f)	B.	Bloomfield	73	115	
1882	1622	Netterville	V.	Netterville	74	116	
1883	1771	Rokeby	B.	Robinson	75	117	
1885	1628	Ranelagh	V.	Jones	76	118	
				Total in 1887 ...	76	118	8

TABLE V.

Peerages which existed *separately* at the time of the Union (1 Jany. 1801), but which have since *merged* into higher or more ancient titles, arranged chronologically according to date of merger, to 31 December 1887.

Date of merger.	Date of creation.	Title of Peerage.	Rank of Peerage.	Surname of First Peer.	Merged into	Number.
1804	1795	Kilwarden of Kilteel	B.	Wolfe	The Viscountcy of Kilwarden(g)	1
1807	1785	Wicklow	V.	Howard	„ Earldom of Wicklow	2
1818	1753	Shelburne	E.	Fitzmaurice-Petty	„ Earldom of Kerry, cr. 1722	3
1831	1797	Ferrard (h)	V.	Foster	„ Viscountcy of Massereene, cr. 1660(h)	4
„	1800	Norbury	B.	Toler	„ Barony of Norwood, cr. 1797	5
1832	1797	Norwood, &c.	B.	„	„ Earldom of Norbury	6
1841	1770	Arden	B.	Perceval	„ Earldom of Egmont	7
1869	1800	Erris (afterwards, 1806, "*promoted*" to the Viscountcy of Lorton)	B.	King	„ Earldom of Kingston	8

Total number, in 1887, of peerages *merged*, 8 ; of which *one* (Kilwarden) has been already reckoned (1830) among the extinctions.

TABLE VI.

Peerages *created* since the Union to 31 Dec. 1887, with the names of the three Peerages on whose extinction they were created in accordance with the act of the Union ; arranged chronologically.

On the extinction of

I. 1806 Feb. 1. Peter Isaac Thellusson, Esq., cr. BARON RENDLESHAM. $\begin{cases} \text{Bateman} & \text{V.} \\ \text{Ross} & \text{E.} \\ \text{Holmes} & \text{B.} \end{cases}$

(a) (b) (c) (d) See notes to commencement of this table.
(e) The Barony of Trimlesdon is, not improbably, only dormant.
(f) See last page note " e."
(g) Both peerages extinct together in 1830.
(h) This merger may, however, not be permanent, inasmuch as the Viscountcy of 1797 descends to heirs *male*, while that of 1660 descends to heirs *general*, of the body of the respective grantees.

II.	1810 May 18. John Prendergast-Smyth, Esq., cr. BARON KILTARTON, with a rem. extended to his nephew Charles Vereker. He was 22 Jany. 1816, cr. VISCOUNT GORT, by "promotion," with a like remainder	Macartney E. Lavington B. Penrhyn B.
III.	1812 Dec. 21. The Rt. Hon. William Handcock, cr. BARON CASTLEMAINE,(a) with a rem. extended to his brother Richard Handcock.	Pery V. Milton B. Delaval B.
IV.	1812 Dec. 21. William Beresford, Archbishop of Tuam, cr. BARON DECIES	Lecale B. Fermanagh B. Longueville V.
V.	1818 Oct. 28. George Canning, Esq., cr. BARON GARVAGH	Belvidere E. Howe V. Callan B.
VI.	1819 Oct. 19. Sir John Francis Cradock, G.C.B., cr. BARON HOWDEN [extinct, 1873]	Cullen V. Upper Ossory E. Sunderlin B.
VII.	1822 Dec. 10. William Downes, Esq., cr. BARON DOWNES, with an extended rem. to his cousin Sir Ulysses Burgh. K.C.B. [extinct, 1863]	Dublin E. Tyrawly B. Tara B.
VIII.	1825 May 14. Sir Benjamin Bloomfield, G.C.B., cr. BARON BLOOMFIELD [extinct, 1879]	Roscommon (b)E. Bulkeley V. Glenbervie B.
IX.	1826 June 27. Catherine, wife of the Rt. Hon. James FitzGerald, cr. BARONESS FITZGERALD AND VESEY, with rem. of that Barony to the heirs male of her body [extinct, 1860]	Milford B. Coleraine B. Eardley B.
X.	1827 June 28. John (Toler), Baron Norbury [I.], cr. EARL OF NORBURY, with a spec. rem. (passing over his eldest son) to his second son,(d) Hector John Toler	Newcomen (c)B. Whitworth B. Carleton V.
XI.	1831 Jany. 28. Standish O'Grady, Chief Baron of the Exchequer, cr. VISCOUNT GUILLAMORE	Ulster E. Castlecoote B. Barrymore E. Carhampton (b)E.
XII.	1831 May 26. Margaret, widow of Richard Talbot, Esq., cr. BARONESS TALBOT OF MALAHIDE, with rem. of that Barony to the heirs male of her body	Mountjoy (e)V. Fortescue V. Kilwarden V.
XIII.	1834 June 13. Robert Shapland Carew, Esq., cr. BARON CAREW	Brandon B. Fitzwilliam V. Llandaf E.
XIV.(g)	1836 May 4. The Rt. Hon. Dominick Browne, cr. BARON ORANMORE AND BROWNE	Munster (f)E. Kingsland V. Connaught E.

(a) He was "promoted." 12 Jany. 1822 to the Viscountcy of Castlemaine, without such extended rem. which Viscountcy, accordingly became extinct on his death, in 1839.

(b) The Earldom of Roscommon was supposed to have become extinct in 1816, and was accordingly used as an extinction in 1825 at the creation of Baron Bloomfield. It was, however, claimed and allowed in 1828. This case had been provided for by the Act of Union, by requiring four extinctions (instead of three) to be used at the next creation. Four extinctions (of which "Carhampton" was the additional one) were accordingly used in 1831 at the creation of Viscount Guillamore, whose (promised) Peerage was thereby delayed for some two years.

(c) The Viscountcy of Newcomen, extinct therewith, was a "promotion."

(d) This spec. rem., which, at the grantee's death, increased the number of Irish Peers, made it necessary to grant the Earldom as a creation, instead of (by the then custom) as a "promotion."

(e) The Earldom of Blesington, extinct therewith, was a "promotion."

(f) The Earldom of Munster, here used as an extinction, had merged in the Crown on the accession thereto of King William IV, 26 June 1830.

(g) The return of the extinctions used thus far, is given from the official returns of Ulster King of Arms, to the House of Lords.

XV. 1845 June 6. James Daly, Esq., *cr.* BARON DUNSANDLE AND CLANCONAL	St. Helens	B.
	Ludlow	E.
	Athlone	E.
XVI. 1848 July 17. The Rt. Hon. Sir Patrick Bellew, Bart., *cr.* BARON BELLEW OF BARMEATH	Hartland	B.
	Allen	V.
	MountSandford	B.
XVII. 1852 Feb. 11. Thomas Fortescue, Esq., *cr.* BARON CLERMONT, with an extended rem. to his brother Chichester Samuel Parkinson-Fortescue	Rancliffe	B.
	Nugent	B.
	Roscommon	E.
XVIII.([a])1856 Sep. 10. Edmund Burke Roche, Esq., *cr.* BARON FERMOY	Tyrconnel	E.
	Melbourne	V.
	Mountrath	E.
	(*for which O'Neill was substituted at the next creation*)([b])	
XIX. 1863 Dec. 14. The Rt. Hon. Sir William Meredyth Somerville, Bart., *cr.* BARON ATHLUMNEY.	O'Neill	V.
	Caher	([c])B.
	Riversdale	B.
	Dungannon	V.
XX. 1868 Dec. 21. John Mc Clintock, Esq., *cr.* BARON RATHDONNEL, with an extended rem. to the heirs male of the body of his late brother William Bunbury Mc Clintock-Bunbury.	Clare	E.
	Palmerston	V.
	Keith	B.

Total of *creations* 20, of which but 16 were existing in 1887.

TABLE VII.

" *Promotions* " (*i.e.* Peerages, of a *higher* grade, conferred on those who already held a Peerage) made since the Union to 31 Dec. 1887 ; arranged chronologically.

1803, Jan.	Limerick, V. (*Pery*), " *promoted* " to the EARLDOM OF LIMERICK.		
„ „	Newcomen, B. (*Newcomen*)	„	VISCOUNTCY OF NEWCOMEN ; *ex.* 1825.
„ Feb.	Dunlo, V. (*Trench*)	„	EARLDOM OF CLANCARTY.
1806, Feb.	Gosford, V. (*Acheson*)	„	„ GOSFORD.
„ „	Oxmantown, B.([d]) (*Parsons*)	„	„ ROSSE.
„ „	Somerton, V. (*Agar*)	„	„ NORMANTON.
„ „	Charleville, V. (*Bury*)	„	„ CHARLEVILLE ; *ex.* 1875.
„ „	Templetown, B. (*Upton*)	„	VISCOUNTCY OF TEMPLETOWN.
„ May.	Lismore, B. (*O'Callaghan*)	„	„ LISMORE.
„ „	Erris, B. (*King*)	„	„ LORTON, which, in 1869, became *merged* in the Earldom of Kingston.
1816, Jan.	Ormonde, E. (*Butler*) " *promoted* " to the MARQUESSATE OF ORMONDE ; *ex.* 1820.		
„ „	Londonderry, E. (*Stewart*)	„	MARQUESSATE OF LONDONDERRY.
„ „	Conyngham, E. (*Conyngham*)	„	„ CONYNGHAM.
„ „	Mountjoy, V. (*Gardiner*)	„	EARLDOM OF BLESINGTON ; *ex.* 1829.
„ „	Bantry, V. (*White*)	„	„ BANTRY.
„ „	Caher, B. (*Butler*)	„	„ GLENGALL;*ex.*1858
„ „	Sheffield, B. (*Holroyd*)	„	„ SHEFFIELD.

([a]) The extinctions used for this and the subsequent creations are kindly furnished by Ulster King of Arms.

([b]) For the reason of this substitution (the extinction of the Earldom of Mountrath not being held to be an extinction of the kind meant by the act of Union). See, *ante*, under " THE FERMOY CASE."

([c]) The *Earldom of Glengall*, extinct therewith was a " promotion."

([d]) The holder of this peerage was himself *Viscount* Oxmantown ; it was, however his *Barony*, which had a *spec. rem.* (not the *Viscountcy*, which became *extinct* at his death in 1807) that was " promoted " into an Earldom.

1816, Jan.	Frankfort, B. (*Morres*)	„	VISCOUNTCY OF FRANKFORT.
„ „	Adare, B. (*Quin*)	„	„ „ MOUNTEARL,
	which, in 1822, became *merged* in the Earldom of Dunraven.		
„ „	Ennismore, B. (*Hare*), "*promoted*" to the VISCOUNTCY OF ENNISMORE AND LISTOWEL, which, in 1822, became *merged* in the Earldom of Listowel.		
„ „	Kiltarton, B. (*Smyth*), "*promoted*" to the VISCOUNTCY OF GORT.		
1822, Feb.	Westmeath, E. (*Nugent*)	„	MARQUESSATE OF WESTMEATH; *c.c.* 1871.
„ „	Kilmorey, V. (*Needham*)	„	EARLDOM OF KILMOREY.
„ „	Monck, V. (*Monck*)	„	„ RATHDOWNE, *ex.* 1849.
„ „	Mountearl, V. (*Quin*)	„	EARLDOM OF DUNRAVEN.
„ „	Ennismore, V. (*Hare*)	„	„ LISTOWEL.
„ „	Castlemaine, B. (*Handcock*)	„	VISCOUNTCY OF CASTLEMAINE; *ex.* 1839.
1825, Oct.	Ormonde, E. (*Butler*)	„	MARQUESSATE OF ORMONDE.
„ Nov.	Clanricarde, E. (*De Burgh*)	„	„ CLANRICARDE.
1831, Sep.	Northland, V. (*Knox*)	„	EARLDOM OF RANFURLY.
1868, Aug.	Strabane, V. (*Hamilton*)	„	DUKEDOM OF ABERCORN.

Total of "*promotions*," 31, of which all, but two, were made by George III and George IV ; the 2 exceptions being an Earldom made by William IV (at his coronation) and a Dukedom made (after an interval of nearly *forty years* !) by Queen Victoria. The whole consists of 9 Viscountcies (whereof 2 are *extinct* and 3 are *merged*) ; 15 Earldoms (whereof 4 are *extinct*) ; 6 Marquessates (whereof 2 are *extinct*) and one Dukedom. Total existing in 1887 (deducting the *merged* as well as the *extinct*) 20.

TABLE VIII.

Peerages which at the time of the Union were united with Peerages of England or of Great Britain, as also Peerages which since that date have become united therewith, or with Peerages of the United Kingdom, arranged chronologically in the order of such their Union.

Date.	Peerage of Ireland.	Peerage of England, G.B., or U.K.	Number.	
			In 1801	In 1887
1447	Waterford, E. (*Talbot*), cr. 1447	Shrewsbury, E., cr. 1442	1	1
1675[a]	Desmond, E. (*Feilding*), cr. 1622	Denbigh, E., cr. 1622	2	2
1681	Lumley, V. (*Lumley*), cr. 1628	Lumley, B., cr. 1681 / Scarbrough, E., cr. 1689	3	3
1689	Cholmondeley, V. (*Cholmondeley*), cr. 1661	Cholmondeley, B., cr. 1689 / „ E., cr. 1706 / „ M., cr. 1815	4	4
1711	Cork, E. (*Boyle*), cr. 1620	Boyle, B., cr. 1711	5	5
1712	Conway, B. (*Seymour-Conway*), cr. 1712	Conway of Ragley, B. cr.1703 / Hertford, E., cr. 1750 / „ M., cr. 1793	6	6
1714	Sherard,[b] B. (*Sherard*), cr. 1627	Harborough, B., cr.1714 / „ E., cr. 1719 *e.c.* 1859	7	(b)

(a) On the death of Basil, 2nd Earl of Denbigh (E.) 28 Nov. 1675, that Earldom devolved on his nephew William, the 2nd Earl of Desmond.

(b) The Barony of Sherard and the Viscountcy of Downe, are the only Irish Peerages *still* (1887) *existing*, which at the time of the Union, were held with Peerages of Great Britain, but which are now Peerages of Ireland *alone*.

Date.	Peerage of Ireland.	Peerage of England, G. B., or U. K.	Number. In 1801	Number. In 1887
1728[a]	Darnley, E. (*Bligh*), cr. 1725	Clifton, B., cr. 1608	8	7
1742	Fitzwilliam, E. (*Fitzwilliam*), cr. 1716	{ Fitzwilliam, B., cr. 1742 „ E., cr. 1743 }	9	8
1747	{ Kildare, E. (*FitzGerald*),cr.1316 Leinster, D. „ cr.1766 }	Leinster, V., cr. 1747	10	9
1749	Bessborough, E. (*Ponsonby*), cr. 1739	Ponsonby, B., cr. 1749	11	10
1756	{ Hillsborough,E.(*Hill*),cr.1751 Downshire, M. „ cr. 1789 }	{ Harwich, B., cr. 1756 Hillsborough, E., cr. 1772 }	12	11
1760	Shelburne,([b]) E. (*Fitzmaurice-Petty*), cr. 1753 ; *merged* 1818([b])	{ Wycombe, B., cr., 1760 Lansdowne, M., cr. 1784 }	13	12
1762	Egmont, E. (*Perceval*), cr. 1733	Lovel and Holland, B., cr. 1762	14	13
„	Milton, B. (*Damer*), cr. 1753 ; *ex.* 1808	{ Milton, B., cr. 1762 „ ex. Dorchester, E., cr. 1792 } 1808	15	—
1764	Connaught, E. (*H.R.H. Prince William-Henry*), cr. 1764 ; *ex.* 1834	Gloucester, D., cr. 1764 ; *ex.* 1834	16	—
1765	Digby, B. (*Digby*), cr. 1620	{ Digby, B., cr. 1765 „ E., cr. 1790; *ex.* 1856 }	17	14
1766[c]	Grandison, V. (*St. John* afterwards *Villiers*), cr. 1621	Jersey, E. (*Villiers*), cr. 1697	18	15
1784	Bulkeley, V. (*Bulkeley*), cr. 1644 ; *ex.* 1822	Bulkeley, B., cr. 1784 ; *ex.* 1822	19	—
„	Ulster, E. (*H.R.H. Prince Frederick*), cr. 1784 ; *ex.* 1827	York, D., cr. 1784 ; *ex.* 1827	20	—
1786	{ Strabane,([d]) V. (*Hamilton*), cr. 1701 Abercorn, D. „ cr. 1868 }	{ Hamilton, V., cr. 1786 Abercorn. M., cr. 1790 }	21	16
„	{ Tyrone, E. (*Beresford*),cr.1746 Waterford, M. „ cr. 1789 }	Tyrone, B., cr. 1786	22	17
„	Shannon, E. (*Boyle*) cr. 1756	Carleton, B., cr. 1786	23	18
„	Delaval, B. (*Delaval*), cr. 1783 ; *ex.* 1808	Delaval, B., cr. 1786; *ex.* 1808	24	—
1788[c]	Nugent, E. (*Nugent*, afterwards *Grenville*), cr. 1776, with a spec. rem.	{ Buckingham, M. (*Grenville*), cr. 1784 Buckingham, D. „ cr. 1822 }	25	19
1789	Munster, E. (*H.R.H. Prince William*), cr. 1789 ; *merged* in the Crown, 1830	Clarence, D., cr. 1789 ; *merged* in the Crown, 1830	26	—
1790	{ Donegall,E.(*Chichester*)cr.1647 M. „ cr.1791 }	Fisherwick, B., cr. 1790	27	20
„	Fife,([f]) E. (*Duff*), cr. 1759	Fife, B., cr. 1790 ; *ex.* 1809	28	([f])

([a]) In 1728, Lord Clifton (E.), who in 1722 had inherited that Barony from his mother, succeeded his father as Earl of Darnley,

([b]) On 4 July 1818, the Irish Earldom of Shelburne (1753) became merged in that of Kerry, cr. 1722.

([c]) On 14 May 1766, by the extinction of the senior line of the Viscounts Grandison, that title devolved on the Earls of Jersey (E.), descended from the youngest brother of the 2d, 3d and 4th Viscounts.

([d]) Earl of Abercorn in Scotland, cr. 1606.

([e]) By the death of Earl Nugent, 14 Oct. 1788, that title devolved on his son-in-law, the Marquess of Buckingham (G.B.).

([f]) Another Barony of Fife (U.K.), was conferred on the holder of this Earldom in 1827, but it, also, became extinct in 1857, in which same year, however, his successor the 5th Earl, was cr. Baron Skene (U.K.).

Date.	Peerage of Ireland.	Peerage of England, G. B., or U. K.	In 1801	In 1887
1790	Grimston, V. (*Grimston*), cr. 1719	{ Verulam, B., cr. 1790 " E., cr. 1815 }	29	21
,	Gage, V. (*Gage*), cr. 1720	Gage B., cr. 1790 (a)	30	22
1793	Auckland, B. (*Eden*), cr. 1789	Auckland, B., cr. 1793	31	23
„ (b)	Moira, E. (*Rawdon* afterwards *Rawdon-Hastings*), cr. 1762 ; ex. 1868	{ Rawdon, B., cr. 1783 } ex. { Hastings, M., cr. 1815 } 1868	32	—
1794	Upper Ossory, E. (*Fitzpatrick*), cr. 1751 ; e.c. 1818	Upper Ossory, B., cr. 1794 ; ex. 1818	33	—
,.	Clive, B. (*Clive*, afterwards *Herbert*), cr. 1762	{ Clive, B., cr. 1794 } { Powis, E., cr. 1804 }	34	24
„	Mulgrave, B. (*Phipps*), cr. 1767	{ Mulgrave, B., cr. 1794 } { „ E., cr. 1812 } { Normanby, M., cr. 1838 }	35	25
„	Westcote, B. (*Lyttelton*), cr. 1776	Lyttelton, B., cr. 1794	36	26
1796	Hood, B. (*Hood*), cr. 1782	Hood, V., cr. 1796	37	27
„	Courtown, E. (*Stopford*), cr. 1762	Saltersford, B., cr 1796	38	28
„	Macartney, E. (*Macartney*), cr. 1794 ; ex. 1806	Macartney, B., cr. 1796 ; ex. 1806	39	—
.,	Downe, (c) V. (*Dawnay*), cr. 1680	Dawnay, B., cr. 1796 ; ex. 1832	40	(c)
„	Midleton, V. (*Brodrick*), cr. 1717	Brodrick, B., cr. 1796	41	29
„	Bridport, (d) B. (*Hood*), cr. 1794	{ Bridport, B., cr. 1796 } cr. 1814 { „ V., cr. 1800 }	42	(d)
1797	{ Mornington, (e) E. (*Wellesley*), cr. 1760 { Wellesley, M. „ cr. 1799 ; ex. 1842	Wellesley, B., cr. 1797; ex. 1842	43	(e)
„	Carrington, B. (*Smith*), cr. 1796	Carrington, B., cr. 1797	44	30
1799	Dublin, E. (*H.R.H. Prince Edward*), cr. 1799 ; ex. 1820	Kent, D., cr. 1799 ; ex. 1820	45	—
„	Armagh, E. (*H.R.H. Prince Ernest*), cr. 1799	Cumberland, D., cr. 1799	46	31
„	Clare, E. (*FitzGibbon*), cr. 1795 ; e.c. 1864	FitzGibbon, B., cr. 1799 ; ex. 1864	47	—
		TOTAL ...	47	31

SINCE THE UNION, 1 JANUARY 1801.

Date.	Peerage of Ireland.	Peerage of England, G. B., or U. K.	In all.	1887
1801	Drogheda, M. (*Moore*), cr. 1791	Moore, B., cr. 1801	1	1
	Ely, M. (*Loftus*), cr. 1800	Loftus, B., cr. 1801	2	2
„	{ Ossory and Ormonde, (f) E. (*Butler*), cr. 1528 and 1541 { Ormonde, M., (*Butler*), cr. 1816 ; e.c. 1820	Butler, B., cr. 1801 ; e.c. 1820	3	(f)

a. A previous Barony of Gage (G. B.) had been conferred in 1780 on this grantee, which became extinct at his death in 1791.

(b) By the death, 20 June 1793, of the 1st Earl of Moira, that Earldom devolved on his son, who had previously, 1783, been cr. Baron Rawdon in Great Britain. He was subsequently, 1815, cr. Marquess of Hastings (U.K.).

(c) See two pages back, note " b."

(d) Another Peerage of Bridport (U.K.), i.e. the *Viscounty* of Bridport, was in 1868, conferred on the holder of this Barony.

(e) The Irish Earldom of Mornington, devolved 26 Sep. 1842, on the Barony of Maryborough (U.K.), and subsequently, 25 July 1863, on the Dukedom of Wellington (U.K.)

(f) Another Peerage U.K., i.e. the Barony of Ormonde, was, in 1821, conferred on the holder of these Earldoms.

Date.	Peerage of Ireland.	Peerage of England, G. B., or U. K.	Number.	
			In all.	In 1887
1801	Carysfort, E. (*Proby*), cr. 1789	Carysfort, B., cr. 1801	4	3
„	St. Helens, B. (*Fitzherbert*), cr. 1791 ; cr. 1839	St. Helens, B., cr. 1801 ; cr. 1839	5	—
„	Thomond, M. (*O'Brien*), cr. 1800; cr. 1855	Thomond, B., cr. 1801 ; cr. 1808	6	—
„	Keith, B. (*Keith-Elphinstone*), cr. 1797 ; cr. 1867	{ Keith of Stonehaven, B. cr. 1801 ; cr. 1823 / Keith of Banheath, B. cr. 1803 ; cr. 1867 \ Keith, V. cr. 1814 ; cr. 1823 }	7	—
1802ᵃ	Clifden, V. (*Agar* afterwards *Agar-Ellis*), cr. 1781	Mendip, B. (*Ellis*), cr. 1794(ᵃ)	8	4
„	Arden, B. (*Perceval*), cr. 1770 ; merged, 1874(ᵇ)	Arden, B., cr. 1802 ; merged 1874(ᵇ)	9	merged ᵇ
„	{ Sheffield, B. (*Holroyd*), cr. 1781 \ „ E. „ cr. 1816 }	Sheffield, B., cr. 1802	10	5
1806	Sligo, M. (*Browne*), cr. 1800	Monteagle, B., cr. 1806	11	6
„	Granard, E. (*Forbes*), cr. 1684	Granard, B., cr. 1806	12	7
„	Gardner, B. (*Gardner*), cr. 1800	Gardner, B., cr. 1806	13	8
1813	Whitworth, B. (*Whitworth*), cr. 1800 ; cr. 1825	{ Whitworth, V., cr. 1813 } cr. \ „ E., cr. 1815 } 1825	14	—
1815	Clancarty, E. (*Trench*), cr. 1803	{ Trench, B., cr. 1815 } \ Clancarty, V., cr. 1823 }	15	9
„	Enniskillen, E. (*Cole*), cr. 1789	Grinstead, B., cr. 1815	16	10
„	Melbourne, V. (*Lamb*), cr. 1781 ; cr. 1853	Melbourne, B., cr. 1815 ; cr. 1853	17	—
1816	Limerick, E. (*Pery*), cr. 1803	Foxford, B., cr. 1815	18	11
1821	Donoughmore, E. (*Hutchinson*), cr. 1800	Hutchinson, V., cr. 1821	19	12
„	Conyngham, M. (*Conyngham*), cr. 1816	Minster, B., cr. 1821	20	13
„	{ Ossory and Ormonde, E. (*Butler*), cr. 1528 and 1541 \ Ormonde, M. (*Butler*), cr. 1825 }	Ormonde, B., cr. 1821	21	14
„	Roden, E. (*Jocelyn*), cr. 1771	Clanbrassil, B., cr. 1821	22	15
„	Kingston, E. (*King*), cr. 1768	Kingston, B., cr. 1821 ; cr. 1869	23	—
„	Longford, E. (*Pakenham*), cr. 1735	Silchester, B., cr. 1821	24	16
1822ᶜ	Londonderry, M. (*Stewart*), cr. 1816	{ Stewart, B., cr. 1814(ᶜ) } \ Vane, E., cr. 1823 }	25	17
1825	Strangford, V. (*Smythe*), cr. 1628; cr. 1869	Penshurt, B., cr. 1825 ; cr. 1869	26	—
,	Thomond, M. (*O'Brien*), cr. 1800 ; cr. 1855	Tadcaster, B., cr. 1826 ; cr. 1846	27	—
„	Clanricarde, M. (*de Burgh*), cr. 1825	Somerhill, B., cr. 1826	28	18

(ᵃ) On 2 Feb. 1802, by the death of Welbore (*Ellis*), 1st Baron Mendip (G.B.), that Barony devolved on his grand-nephew, Henry Welbore (*Agar*), 2d Viscount Clifden.
(ᵇ) On 2 Aug. 1874, the Irish Barony of Arden, *merged* in the Earldom of Egmont : and the Barony of Arden (U.K.), merged in the Barony of Lovel and Holland cr. 1762.
(ᶜ) On 12 Aug. 1822 by the death of Robert, 2nd Marquess of Londonderry, that title devolved on his brother Charles, Baron Stewart, (U.K.).

Date.	Peerage of Ireland.	Peerage of England, G. B., or U. K.	Number. In all.	Number. In 1887
1825	{ Northland, V. (*Knox*), cr. 1791 } { Ranfurly, E. „ cr. 1831 }	Ranfurly, B., cr. 1826	29	19
1827	Fife,(a) E. (*Duff*), cr. 1759	Fife, B., cr. 1827 ; ex. 1857	30	(a)
1828	Clanwilliam, E. (*Meade*), cr. 1776	Clanwilliam, B., cr. 1828	31	20
1828b	Ferrard, V. (*Foster*), cr. 1797 ; merged 1843(b)	Oriel, B., cr. 1821(b)	32	(b)
1831	Fingall, E. (*Plunkett*), cr. 1628	Fingall, B., cr. 1831	33	21
„	Sefton, E. (*Molyneux*), cr. 1771	Sefton, B., cr. 1831	34	22
„	Leitrim, E. (*Clements*), cr. 1795	Clements, B., cr. 1831	35	23
„	Headfort, M. (*Taylor*), cr. 1800	Kenlis, B., cr. 1831	36	24
„	Meath, E. (*Brabazon*), cr. 1627	Chaworth, B., cr, 1831	37	25
„	Ludlow, E. (*Ludlow*), cr. 1760 ; ex. 1842	Ludlow, B., cr. 1831 ; ex. 1842	38	—
„	Howden, B. (*Cradock*), cr. 1819 ; ex. 1873	Howden, B., cr. 1831 ; ex. 1873	39	—
„	Cloncurry, B. (*Lawless*), cr. 1789	Cloncurry, B., cr. 1831	40	'26
1835	FitzGerald and Vesey, B. (*FitzGerald*), cr. 1826 ; ex. 1860	FitzGerald, B., cr. 1835 ; ex. 1843	41	—
„	Gosford, E. (*Acheson*), cr. 1806	Worlingham, B., cr. 1835	42	27
1837	Charlemont, E. (*Caulfield*), cr. 1763	Charlemont, B., cr. 1837	43	28
1838	Lismore, V. (*O'Callagan*), cr. 1806	Lismore, B., cr. 1838	44	29
„	Rossmore, B. (*Cuninghame* afterwards *Westenra*), cr. 1796	Rossmore, B., cr. 1838	45	30
„	Carew, B. (*Carew*), cr. 1834	Carew, B., cr. 1838	46	31
1839	Talbot of Malahide,(c) B. (*Talbot*), cr. 1831	Furnival, B., cr. 1839 ; ex. 1849	47	(c)
1841	Kenmare,(c) E. (*Browne*), cr. 1800	Kenmare, B., cr. 1841; ex. 1853	48	(c)
1842d	Mornington, E. (*Wellesley*), cr. 1760(d)	Maryborough, B., cr. 1821 ; ex. 1863	49	—
1843b	Massereene,V.(*Skeffington*),cr. 1660	Oriel, B., cr. 1821b	50	32
1847	Cremorne, B. (*Dawson*), cr. 1797	{ Dartrey, B., cr. 1847 } { „ E., cr. 1866 }	51	33
1850	Dufferin and Clandeboye, B. (*Blackwood*), cr. 1800	{ Clandeboye, B., cr. 1850 } { Dufferin, E., cr. 1871 }	52	34
1856e	Kenmare, E. (*Browne*). cr. 1800(e)	Kenmare, B., cr. 1856	53	35
„ f	Talbot of Malahide, B. (*Talbot*), cr. 1831(f)	Talbot de Malahide, B., cr. 1856	54	36
1857a	Fife, E. (*Duff*, cr. 1759(a)	{ Skene, B., cr. 1857 } { Fife, E., cr. 1885 }	55	37
1863d	Mornington, E. (*Wellesley*), cr. 1760(d)	Wellington, D., cr. 1814	56	38
1866g	Clermont, B.(*Fortescue*),cr. 1852(g)	Clermont, B., cr. 1866; ex. 1887	57	(g)

(a) See three pages back, note "f."

(b) On 16 Aug. 1828 by the death of John, (*Foster*) 1st Baron Oriel, (U. K.) that title devolved on his son Thomas Henry, Viscount Ferrard, who, on 20 Jan. 1824, had succeeded his mother in that Viscountcy. Viscount Ferrard married Harriet, *suo jure* Viscountess Massereene (a creation of 1660) in which Peerage the Viscountcy of Ferrard (1797) became merged (when inherited by his son then Viscount Massereene) on his death in 1843. See, however, note "b" to Table III.

(c) Another Barony (U.K.), was in 1856 conferred on the holder of this Peerage.

(d) See two pages back, note "e."

(e) A previous Barony of Kenmare (U. K.) had, in 1841, been conferred on the holder of this Earldom.

(f) A previous Barony (U. K.), that of *Furnival*, had, in 1839, been conferred on the holder of this Peerage.

(g) See next page, note "a."

Date.	Peerage of Ireland.	Peerage of England, G. B., or U. K.	Number. In all.	In 1887
1866	Athlumney, B. (Somerville), cr. 1863	Meredyth, B., cr. 1866	58	39
„	Dunraven and Mount Earl, E. (Quin, afterwards Wyndham-Quin), cr. 1822	Kenry, B., cr. 1866	59	40
„	Monck, V. (Monck), cr. 1801	Monck, B., cr. 1866	60	41
„	Henniker, B. (Henniker afterwards Henniker-Major) cr. 1800	Hartismere, B., cr. 1866	61	42
„	Boyne, V. (Hamilton), cr. 1717	Brancepeth. B., cr. 1866	62	43
1868	Bridport, B. (Hood), cr. 1794	Bridport, V., cr. 1868	63	44
„	Gormanston, V. (Preston) cr. 1478	Gormanston, B., cr. 1868	64	45
1869	Listowel, E. (Hare), cr. 1827	Hare, B., cr. 1869	65	46
1871	Bloomfield, B. (Bloomfield) cr. 1825 ; ex. 1879	Bloomfield, B., cr. 1871 ; ex. 1879	66	—
1873	Normanton, E. (Agar), cr. 1806	Somerton, B., cr. 1873	67	47
1876	Erne, E. (Crichton), cr. 1789	Fermanagh, B., cr. 1876	68	48
1880	Barrington, V. (Barrington) cr. 1720	Shute, B., cr. 1880	69	49
1881	Howth, E. (St. Lawrence), cr. 1767	Howth, B., cr. 1881	70	50
1884	Arran, E. (Gore), cr. 1762	Sudley, B., cr. 1884	71	51
„	De Vesci, V. (Vesey), cr. 1776	De Vesci, B., cr. 1884	72	52
1885	Powerscourt, V. (Wingfield), cr. 1743	Powerscourt, B., cr. 1885	73	53
„	Henley, B. (Eden afterwards Henley), cr. 1799	Northington, B., cr. 1885	74	54
1886	Hawarden, V. (Maude), er. 1793	De Montalt, E., cr. 1886	75	55
„	Kensington, B. (Edwardes), cr. 1776	Kensington, B., cr. 1886	76	56
1887	Galway, V. (Monckton, afterwards Monckton-Arundell), cr. 1727	Monckton, B., cr. 1887	77	57
„ (a)	Clermont, B. (Fortescue), cr. 1852(a)	Carlingford, B., cr. 1874	78	58
	Total of Peerages which, since the Union, have become united with Peerages of England, Great Britain, or the United Kingdom ... **1135678**		78	
	Ditto of such still so existing in 1887 ...			58
	To which add the Peerages which at the time of the Union were united with Peerages of England or Great Britain, and which, in 1887, still so continue. (See three pages back in second column)			31
	Total of Peerages, which, in 1887, were united with Peerages of England, Great Britain or the United Kingdom ...			89

Note.—On 3 May 1870, Charles William FitzGerald, styled Marquess of Kildare, s. and h. ap. of the Duke of Leinster, was cr. Baron Kildare [U.K.], but that title merged in the Viscountcy of Leinster, cr. 1747 (see Table viii) on 10 Oct. 1874, when, on the death of his Father, he inherited the Irish honours of his family, together with the said Viscountcy.

(a) On 29 July 1887, by the death of Lord Clermont (I. and U. K.), the Irish Barony (alone) of that name (cr. 1852). devolved on his brother Lord Carlingford (U. K.). the Barony of Clermont [U.K.], cr. 1866, becoming extinct.

TABLE IX.

List of Irish Representative Peers since the Union ; arranged chronologically.

The 28 Representative Peers elected at the time of the Union.

1.	1801, Jany. 1.	Thomas (Taylour), 1st MARQUESS OF HEADFORT ; *d.* 24 Oct. 1829.
2.	,,	,,	John Denis (Browne), 1st MARQUESS OF SLIGO ; *cr.* Baron Monteagle [U.K.] 20 Feb. 1806 ; *d.* 2 Jan. 1809.
3.	,,	,,	John Thomas (de Burgh) 13th EARL OF CLANRICARDE ; *d.* 27 July 1808.
4.	,,	,,	George Frederick (Nugent), 7th EARL OF WESTMEATH ; *d.* 30 Dec. 1814.
5.	,,	,,	Robert (Jocelyn), 2nd EARL OF RODEN ; *d.* 29 June 1820.
6.	,,	,,	John (Crosbie), 2nd EARL OF GLANDORE ; *d.* 23 Oct. 1815.
7.	,,	,,	Thomas (Pakenham), 2nd EARL OF LONGFORD ; *cr.* Baron Silchester [U.K.] 17 July 1821 ; *d.* 24 May 1835.
8.	,,	,,	John (Creighton), 1st EARL ERNE ; *d.* 15 Sep. 1828.
9.	,,	,,	Otway (Cuffe), 1st EARL OF DESART ; *d.* 9 Aug. 1804.
10.	,,	,,	Robert (Clements), 1st EARL OF LEITRIM ; *d.* 27 July 1804
11.	,,	,,	Richard (Bingham), 2nd EARL OF LUCAN ; *d.* 30 June 1839.
12.	,,	,,	Robert (Stewart), 1st EARL OF LONDONDERRY ; *pr.* as MARQUESS OF LONDONDERRY, 22 Jan. 1816 ; *d.* 8 April 1821.
13.	,,	,,	Henry (Conyngham), 1st EARL CONYNGHAM ; *pr.* as MARQUESS CONYNGHAM, 22 Jan. 1816 ; *cr.* Baron Minster [U.K.], 17 June 1821 ; *d.* 28 Dec. 1832.
14.	,,	,,	Francis (Mathew), 1st EARL OF LLANDAFF ; *d.* Sep. 1806.
15.	,,	,,	Charles Henry (O'Neill), 1st EARL O'NEILL ; *d.* 25 March 1841.
16.	,,	,,	Francis (Bernard), 1st EARL OF BANDON ; *d.* 26 Nov. 1830.
17.	,,	,,	Richard (Hely-Hutchinson), 1st EARL OF DONOUGHMORE ; *cr.* Viscount Hutchinson [U.K.], 14 June 1821 ; *d.* 22 Aug. 1825.
18.	,,	,,	Robert (Howard), 2nd VISCOUNT WICKLOW ; *suc.* 7 March 1807, as EARL OF WICKLOW ; *d.* 23 Oct. 1815.
19.	,,	,,	Thomas (Knox), 1st VISCOUNT NORTHLAND ; *d.* 5 Nov. 1818.
20.	,,	,,	Laurence (Harman-Parsons), 1st VISCOUNT OXMANTOWN ; *pr.* as EARL OF ROSSE, Feb. 1806 ; *d.* 20 April 1807.
21.	,,	,,	Hugh (Carleton), VISCOUNT CARLETON OF CLARE ; *d.* 25 Feb. 1826.
22.	,,	,,	Edmund Henry (Pery), 1st VISCOUNT LIMERICK ; *pr.* as EARL OF LIMERICK, 11 Feb. 1803 ; *cr.* Baron Foxford [U.K.], 11 Aug. 1815 ; *d.* 7 Dec. 1844.
23.	,,	,,	Charles (Agar), VISCOUNT SOMERTON (Archbishop of Cashel, 1779-1801, and subsequently, 1801-1809, of Dublin) ; *pr.* as EARL OF NORMANTON, 7 Feb. 1806 ; *d.* 14 July 1809.
24.	,,	,,	Richard (Longfield), VISCOUNT LONGUEVILLE ; *d.* 23 May 1811.
25.	,,	,,	Richard (Butler), 10th LORD CAHER ; *pr.* as EARL OF GLENGALL, 22 Jan. 1816 ; *d.* 20 Jan. 1819.
26.	,,	,,	George (Agar), BARON CALLAN ; *d.* 29 Oct. 1815.
27.	,,	,,	Robert (Cuninghame), 1st BARON ROSSMORE ; *d.* 6 Aug. 1801.
28.(a)	,,	,,	James (Cuffe), BARON TYRAWLEY ; *d.* 15 June 1821 (b)

(a) Of the above 28 it is to be observed that no less than 21 had *themselves* obtained a Peerage (*viz.* 20 being the first Peers of their then style and the other, the Earl of Clanricarde, having in 1800 obtained another Earldom with a spec. rem. in favour of his daughter) ; five others (*viz.* Roden, Glandore, Longford, Lucan and Wicklow) were the *sons* of persons who had received peerages, while of the remaining two (1) Caher, subsequently, obtained an Earldom, and the other (2) Westmeath, was posthumously rewarded (as indeed was Clanricarde also) by a Marquessate granted to his son.

(b) Of these Peers all but five (Conyngham, Longford, Lucan, O'Neill and Limerick

29.	1801, Sep. 10.	Charles William (Bury), 1st VISCOUNT CHARLEVILLE, *vice* Baron Rossmore [No. 27]. He was *pr.* as EARL OF CHARLEVILLE, 16 Feb. 1806 ; *d.* 31 Oct. 1835.
30.	1804, Aug. 21.	John Willoughby (Cole), 2nd EARL OF ENNISKILLEN, *vice* the Earl of Leitrim [No. 10]. He was *cr.* Baron Grinstead [U.K.], 11 Aug. 1815 ; *d.* 31 March, 1840.
31.	„ Oct. 3.	Dupré (Alexander), 2nd EARL OF CALEDON, *vice* the 1st Earl of Desart [No. 9]. He *d.* 8 April 1839.
32.	1806, Sep. 30.	Francis William (Caulfeild), 2nd EARL OF CHARLEMONT, *vice* the Earl of Llandaff [No. 14]. He was *cr.* Baron Charlemont [U.K.], 13 Feb. 1837 : *d.* 26 Dec. 1863.
33.	1807, May 19.	George (King), 3rd EARL OF KINGSTON, *vice* the Earl of Rosse [No. 20]. He was *cr.* Baron Kingston [U.K.], 17 July 1821 ; *d.* 18 Oct. 1839.
34.	1808, Oct. 24.	Richard (Le Poer Trench), 2nd EARL OF CLANCARTY, *vice* the Earl of Clanricarde [No. 3]. He was *cr.* Baron Trench [U.K.], 4 Aug. 1815, and Viscount Clancarty [U.K.], 8 Dec. 1823 ; *d.* 24 Nov. 1837.
35.	1809, Feb. 21.	Charles John (Gardiner), 2nd VISCOUNT MOUNTJOY, *vice* the Marquess of Sligo [No. 2]. He was *pr.* as EARL OF BLESINGTON, 22 Jan. 1816 ; *d.* 25 May 1829.
36.	„ Aug. 29.	Laurence (Parsons), 2nd EARL OF ROSSE, *vice* the Earl of Normanton [No. 23]. He *d.* 24 Feb. 1841.
37.	1811, June 27.	Archibald (Acheson), 2nd EARL OF GOSFORD, *vice* Viscount Longueville [No. 24]. He was *cr.* Baron Worlingham [U.K.], 13 June 1835 ; *d.* 27 March 1849.
38.	1815, Jan. 30.	Stephen (Moore), 2nd EARL MOUNTCASHELL, *vice* the Earl of Westmeath [No. 4]. He *d.* 27 Oct. 1822.
39.	1816, Jan. 9.	William (O'Brien), 2nd MARQUESS OF THOMOND, *vice* the Earl of Glandore [No. 6]. He was *cr.* Baron Tadcaster [U.K.], 3 July 1826 ; *d.* 21 Aug. 1846.
40.	„ „	John James (Maxwell), 2nd EARL OF FARNHAM, *vice* the Earl of Wicklow [No. 18]. He *d.* 23 July 1823.
41.	„ „	John (Bourke), 4th EARL OF MAYO, *vice* Baron Callan [No. 26]. He *d.* 23 May 1849.
42.	1819, Jan. 19.	Somerset Richard (Butler), 3rd EARL OF CARRICK, *vice* Viscount Northland [No. 19]. He *d.* 4 Feb. 1838.
43.	„ March 9.	Somerset (Lowry-Corry), 2nd EARL BELMORE, *vice* the Earl of Glengall [No. 25]. He *d.* 18 April 1841.
44.	1820, Aug. 15.	James Stevenson (Blackwood), BARON DUFFERIN AND CLANEBOYE, *vice* the Earl of Roden [No. 5]. He *d.* 8 Aug. 1836.
45.	1821, June(a) 11.	Richard (Wingfield), 5th VISCOUNT POWERSCOURT, *vice* the Marquess of Londonderry [No. 12]. He *d.* 9 Aug. 1823.
46.	„ Sep. 18.	William (Howard), EARL OF WICKLOW, *vice* Baron Tyrawly [No. 28]. He *d.* 22 March 1869.
47.	1822, Dec. 14.	Robert Edward (King), 1st VISCOUNT LORTON, *vice* Earl Mountcashell [No. 38]. He *d.* 20 Nov. 1854.
48.	1823, Sep. 2.	John (Evans-Freke), 6th BARON CARBERY, *vice* the Earl of Farnham [No. 40]. He *d.* 12 May 1845.
49.	„ Oct. 14.	Charles (Vereker), 2nd VISCOUNT GORT, *vice* Viscount Powerscourt [No. 45]. He *d.* 11 Nov. 1842.
50.	1825, Oct. 25.	John (Maxwell), 5th BARON FARNHAM, *vice* the Earl of Doroughmore [No. 17]. He *d.* 19 Oct. 1838.
51.	1826, May 9.	Stephen (Moore), 3rd EARL MOUNTCASHELL, *vice* Viscount Carleton of Clare [No. 21]. He *d.* 10 Oct. 1883.
52.	1828, Oct. 27.	Henry Sadlier (Prittie), 2nd BARON DUNALLEY, *vice* Earl Erne [No. 8]. He *d.* 19 Oct. 1854.

were dead within the next 30 years ; all but two (O'Neill and Limerick) within the next 40 years, the survivor, the Earl of Limerick, dying 7 Dec. 1844 in the 86th year of his age and the 44th of his election.

(a) *January,* according to the Report of 1874, see two pages on, note "a."

53.	1829, July 10.	Richard (Butler), 2nd EARL OF GLENGALL, *vice* the Earl of Blesington [No. 35]. He *d.* 22 June 1858.
54.	1830, Jan. 21.	Hayes (St. Leger), 2nd VISCOUNT DONERAILE, *vice* the Marquess of Headfort [No. 1]. He *d.* 27 March 1854.
55.	1831, Jan. 4.	George Thomas (Nugent), Marquess of Westmeath, *vice* the Earl of Bandon [No. 16]. He *d.* 5 May 1871.
56.	1833, Feb. 5.	Ulysses (De Burgh), 2nd BARON DOWNES, *vice* Marquess Conyngham [No. 13]. He *d.* 26 July 1863.
57.	1835, June 9.	James (Bernard), 2nd EARL OF BANDON, *vice* the Earl of Longford [No. 7]. He *d.* 31 Oct. 1856.
58.	„ Nov. 26.	Edward Wadding (Plunkett), 14th LORD DUNSANY, *vice* the Earl of Charleville [No. 29]. He *d.* 11 Dec. 1848.
59.	1836, Sep. 8.	Cornwallis (Maude), 3rd VISCOUNT HAWARDEN, *vice* Baron Dufferin and Claneboye [No. 44]. He *d.* 12 Oct. 1856.
60.	1837, Dec. 29.	Robert (Dillon), 3rd BARON CLONBROCK, *vice* the Earl of Clancarty [No. 34]. He was *the senior Rep. Peer living* 1889.
61.	1838, Feb. 19.	Charles William (Bury), 2nd EARL OF CHARLEVILLE, *vice* the Earl of Carrick [No. 42]. He *d.* 14 July 1851.
62.	„ Nov. 27.	John (Vesey), 2nd VISCOUNT DE VESCI, *vice* Baron Farnham [No. 50]. He *d.* 19 Oct. 1855.
63.	1839, May 10.	Henry (Maxwell), 7th BARON FARNHAM, *vice* the Earl of Caledon [No. 31]. He *d.* 20 Aug. 1868.
64.	„ July 30.	Wyndham Alexander (Quin), 2nd EARL OF DUNRAVEN AND MOUNTEARL, *vice* the Earl of Lucan [No. 11]. He *d.* 6 Aug. 1850.
65.	„ Nov. 29.	Edward (Crofton), BARON CROFTON OF MOTE, *vice* the Earl of Kingston [No. 33]. He *d.* 27 Oct. 1869.
66.	1840, May 1.	George Charles (Bingham), 3rd EARL OF LUCAN, *vice* the Earl of Enniskillen [No. 30]. He *d.* 10 Nov. 1888.
67.	1841, March 16.	James Du Pré (Alexander), 3rd EARL OF CALEDON, *vice* the Earl of Rosse [No. 36]. He *d.* 30 June 1855.
68.	„ April 20.	Cadwallader Davis (Blayney), 12th BARON BLAYNEY OF MONAGHAN, *vice* Earl O'Neill [No. 15]. He *d.* 18 Jan. 1874.
69.	„ May 14.	Richard (Handcock), 3rd BARON CASTLEMAINE, *vice* Earl Belmore [No. 43]. He *d.* 4 July 1869.
70.	1842, Dec. 9.	John Bruce Richard (O'Neill), 3rd VISCOUNT O'NEILL, *vice* Viscount Gort [No. 49]. He *d.* 12 Feb. 1855.
71.	1845, Jan. 2.	William (Parsons), 3rd EARL OF ROSSE, *vice* the Earl of Limerick [No. 22]. He *d.* 31 Oct. 1867.
72.	„ June 2.	John (Crichton), 3rd EARL ERNE, *vice* Baron Carbery [No. 48]. He *d.* 3 Oct. 1885.
73.	1846, Oct. 20.	John Otway (Cuffe), 3rd EARL OF DESART, *vice* the Marquess of Thomond [No. 39]. He *d* 1 April 1865.
74.	1849, Feb. 23.	Eyre (Massey), 3rd BARON CLARINA, *vice* Lord Dunsany [No. 58]. He *d.* 18 Nov. 1872].
75.	„ May 1.	John Cavendish (Browne), 3rd BARON KILMAINE, *vice* the Earl of Gosford [No. 37]. He *d.* 13 Jan. 1873.
76.	„ June 22.	George John Danvers (Butler-Danvers), EARL OF LANESBOROUGH, *vice* the Earl of Mayo [No. 41]. He *d.* 7 July 1866.
77.	1850, Sep. 27.	Randal Edward (Plunkett), 15th LORD DUNSANY. *vice* the Earl of Dunraven and Mountearl [No. 64]. He *d.* 7 April 1852.
78.	1851, Aug. 1.	Denis St. George (Daly), 2nd BARON DUNSANDLE AND CLANCONAL, *vice* the Earl of Charleville [No. 61]. He was *living* 1889.
79.	1852, April 30.	Robert (Bourke), 5th EARL OF MAYO, *vice* Lord Dunsany [No. 77]. He *d.* 13 Aug. 1867.
80.	1854, May 9.	Richard (White), 2nd EARL OF BANTRY, *vice* Viscount Doneraile [No. 54]. He *d.* 16 July, 1868.
81.	„ Nov. 17.	Edward (Ward), 4th VISCOUNT BANGOR, *vice* Baron Dunalley [No. 52]. He *d.* 14 Sep. 1881.

82.	1855, Jan. 2.	Henry John Reuben (Dawson-Damer), 3rd EARL OF PORT-ARLINGTON, *vice* Viscount Lorton [No. 47]. He was *living* 1889.
83.	„ March 10.	Hayes (St. Leger), 4th VISCOUNT DONERAILE, *vice* Viscount O'Neill [No. 70]. He *d.* 26 Aug. 1887.
84.	„ July 20.	Arthur (Hill-Trevor), 3rd VISCOUNT DUNGANNON, *vice* the Earl of Caledon [No. 67]. He *d.* 11 Aug. 1862.
85.	„ Dec. 1.	James (Hewitt), 4th VISCOUNT LIFFORD, *vice* Viscount De Vesci [No. 62]. He *d.* 20 Nov. 1887.
86.	1856, Nov. 18.	Thomas (Vesey), 3rd VISCOUNT DE VESCI, *vice* Viscount Hawarden [No. 59]. He *d.* 23 Dec. 1875.
87.	„ Nov. 21.	Somerset Richard (Lowry-Corry), 4th EARL BELMORE, *vice* the Earl of Bandon [No. 57]. He was *living* 1889.
88.	1858, June 29.	Francis (Bernard), 3rd EARL OF BANDON, *vice* the Earl of Glengall [No. 53]. He *d.* 17 Feb. 1877.
89.	1862, Oct. 10.	Cornwallis (Maude), 4th VISCOUNT HAWARDEN, *vice* Viscount Dungannon [No. 84]. He was on 9 Sep. 1886, *cr.* Earl de Montalt [U.K.] and was *living* 1889.
90.	1863, Aug. 28.	Lucius (O'Brien), 13th BARON INCHIQUIN, *vice* Baron Downes [No. 56]. He *d.* 22 March 1872.
91.	1864, Jan. 15.	Edward (Plunkett), 16th LORD DUNSANY, *vice* the Earl of Charlemont [No. 32]. He was *living* 1889.
92.	1865, April 21.	John Prendegast (Vereker), 3rd VISCOUNT GORT, *vice* the Earl of Desart [No. 73]. He *d.* 20 Oct. 1865.
93.	„ Nov. 3.	Mervyn (Wingfield), 7th VISCOUNT POWERSCOURT, *vice* Viscount Gort [No. 92]. He was *living* 1889.
94.	1866, July 24.	George Frederick (Upton), 3rd VISCOUNT TEMPLETOWN, *vice* the Earl of Lanesborough [No. 76]. He was *living* 1889.
95.	1867, Aug. 23,	William Richard (Annesley), 4th EARL ANNESLEY, *vice* the Earl of Mayo [No. 79]. He *d.* 10 Aug 1874.
96.	„ Nov. 29.	Theobald Fitzwalter (Butler), 14th BARON DUNBOYNE, *vice* the Earl of Rosse [No. 71]. He *d.* 22 March 1881.
97.	1868, Aug. 4.	Charles Allanson (Winn), 3rd LORD HEADLEY, BARON ALLANSON AND WINN, *vice* the Earl of Bantry [No. 80]. He *d.* 30 July 1877.
98.	„ Oct. 30.	Laurence (Parsons), 4th EARL OF ROSSE, *vice* Baron Farnham [No. 63]. He was *living* 1889.
99.	1869, May 14.	William Henry Hare (White), 3rd EARL OF BANTRY, *vice* the Earl of Wicklow [No. 46]. He *d.* 15 Jan. 1884.
100.	„ July 15.	Geoffrey Dominick Augustus Frederick (Browne-Guthrie) 2nd BARON ORANMORE AND BROWNE, *vice* Baron Castlemaine [No. 69]. He was *living* 1889.
101.	1870, Feb. 11.	John Vansittart Danvers (Butler-Danvers), 6th EARL OF LANESBOROUGH, *vice* Baron Crofton [No. 65]. He was *living* 1889.
102.	1871, May 18.	Dayrolles Blakeney (Eveleigh-De Moleyns), 4th BARON VENTRY, *vice* the Marquess of Westmeath [No. 55]. He was *living* 1889.
103.	1872, April 27.	Charles Francis Arnold (Howard), EARL OF WICKLOW, *vice* Baron Inchiquin [No. 90]. He *d.* 20 June, 1881.
104.	„ Dec. 20.	Edward Henry Churchill (Crofton), BARON CROFTON, *vice* Baron Clarina [No. 74]. He (as were all that have been elected subsequently to him) was *living* 1889.
105.	1873, Feb. 11.	Edward Donough (O'Brien), 14th BARON INCHIQUIN, *vice* Baron Kilmaine [No. 75]
106.	1874, March 17.([a])	Richard (Handcock), 4th BARON CASTLEMAINE, *vice* Baron Blayney of Monaghan [No. 68].
107.	„ Nov. 10.([b])	John Henry Reginald Scott), 4th EARL OF CLONMELL, *vice* Earl Annesley [No. 95].

([a]) The dates to this point are from the Report of the Committee of House of Lords on the REP. PEERAGE of Scotland and Ireland printed 23 July 1874.

([b]) This date and those subsequently have been kindly supplied by Sir A. W. Woods, *Garter*.

108. 1876, March 14. John Thomas William (Massy), 6th BARON MASSY OF DUN-
TRILEAGUE, *vice* Viscount De Vesci [No. **86**].

109. 1877, April 28. Hugh (Annesley), 5th EARL ANNESLEY, *vice* the Earl of
Bandon, [No. **88**].

110. „ Oct. 30. James (Alexander), 4th EARL OF CALEDON, *vice* Lord
Headley [No. **97**].

111. 1881, June 6. James Francis (Bernard), 4th EARL OF BANDON, *vice* Baron
Dunboyne [No. **96**].

112. „ Aug. 23. Edward Nugent (Leeson), 6th EARL OF MILLTOWN, *vice* the
Earl of Wicklow [No. **103**].

113. „ Dec. 31. Francis Charles (Needham), 3rd EARL OF KILMOREY, *vice*
Viscount Bangor [No. **81**].

114. 1883, Dec. 20. Charles Mark Allanson (Winn), 4th LORD HEADLEY, BARON
ALLANSON AND WINN, *vice* Earl Mountcashell [No. **51**].

115. 1884, March 14. Hercules Edward (Rowley), 4th BARON LANGFORD, *vice* the
Earl of Bantry [No. **99**].

116. 1885, Nov. 27. Henry William Crosbie (Ward), 5th VISCOUNT BANGOR, *vice*
Earl Erne [No. **72**].

117. 1887, Oct. 24. Henry Ernest Newcomen (King-Tenison), 8th EARL OF
KINGSTON, *vice* Viscount Doneraile [No. **83**].

118. 1888, Jan. 23. Cecil Ralph (Howard), EARL OF WICKLOW, *vice* Viscount
Lifford, [No. **85**].

119. „ Dec. 31. Eyre Challoner Henry (Massey), 4th BARON CLARINA, *vice*
the Earl of Lucan]No. **66**.]

TABLE X.

List of the KNIGHTS of the most illustrious Order OF ST. PATRICK from the institution
of that Order, 5 Feb. 1783.

[Founded 5 Feb. 1783, the number being limited to 15, exclusive of the *Sovereign*,
and of the Chief-Governor of Ireland for the time being, who, during his term of office,
is *Grand Master*.

In July 1821 six extra Knights were nom. at the coronation of George IV, of which
number, four, during his reign, became subsequently constituent members by the
death of four regularly elected members.

On 18 Nov. 1831, four *more* extra Knights were nom. at the coronation of William
IV, and on 24 Jan. 1833 the total *number* was permanently *increased*, from 15 to 22.

In 1839 Queen Victoria authorised each successive *Grand Master* to retain and wear
the star, riband and badge of the Order, *after* he had ceased to be Chief Governor of
Ireland].

Date of Nomination.	The fifteen original Knights, or "KNIGHTS FOUNDERS," nominated 5 Feb. 1783, were as under; of these, fourteen were *invested* [11 March 1783] and *installed* [17 March 1783], the 15th, the Earl of Ely, being absent from ill health and dying soon afterwards.
1. 1783, Feb. 5.	*H.R.H.* PRINCE EDWARD, afterwards (24 April 1799), *cr.* DUKE OF KENT AND STRATHEARN [G.B.] and EARL OF DUBLIN. He *d* 23 Jan. 1820.
2. „ „	William Robert (Fitz Gerald), 2nd DUKE OF LEINSTER. He *d*. 20 Oct. 1804.
3. „ „	Henry (De Burgh), 12th EARL OF CLANRICARDE, afterwards (18 Aug. 1785), *cr.* MARQUESS OF CLANRICARDE. He *d*. 8 Dec. 1797.
4.(a) „ „	Thomas (Nugent), 6th EARL OF WESTMEATH. He *d*. 7 Sep. 1792.

(a) Randall William (Mac Donnell), 6th EARL OF ANTRIM (who would have been
here placed, between the Earls of Clanricarde and Westmeath) declined the honour,
not wishing to give up the Order of the Bath which was a preliminary required of
him. The Earl of Arran [No. *11*] was consequently elected in his room.

5. 1783, Feb. 5. Murrough (O'Brien), 5th EARL OF INCHIQUIN, afterwards (29 Dec., 1800) cr. MARQUESS OF THOMOND. He d. 10 Feb. 1808.
6. „ „ Charles (Moore), 6th EARL OF DROGHEDA, afterwards (5 July 1791), cr. MARQUESS OF DROGHEDA. He d. 22 Dec. 1821.(b)
7. „ „ George de la Poer (Beresford), 2d EARL OF TYRONE, afterwards (19 Aug. 1789), cr. MARQUESS OF WATERFORD. He d. 3 Dec. 1800.
8. „ „ Richard (Boyle), 2d EARL OF SHANNON. He d. 20 May 1807.
9. „ „ James (Hamilton), 2d EARL OF CLANBRASSILL. He d. 6 Feb. 1798. (Peerage extinct before the Union.)
10. „ „ Richard (Wellesley), 2d EARL OF MORNINGTON, afterwards (20 Oct. 1797), cr. MARQUESS WELLESLEY. He resigned 3 3 March 1810, on being elected K.G.(c)
11. „ March 9.(d) Arthur Saunders (Gore), 2d EARL OF ARRAN.(d) He d. 8 Oct. 1809.
12. „ Feb. 5. James (Stopford), 2d EARL OF COURTOWN. He d. 30 March, 1810.
13. „ „ James (Caulfeild), 1st EARL OF CHARLEMONT. He d. 4 Aug., 1799.
14. „ „ Thomas (Taylour), 1st EARL OF BECTIVE. He d. 14 Feb. 1795.

15. „ „ Henry (Loftus), EARL OF ELY. He d. abroad 8 May 1783, without having ever been invested or installed, and is therefore not considered as one of the Knight's Founders, tho' named in the letters patent. (Peerage extinct before the Union.)

Date of Investiture. *Knights nominated since the foundation.*

16. 1784, Feb. 5.(e) John Joshua (Proby), 2d BARON CARYSFORT, vice the Earl of Ely [No. 15]. He was, on 18 Aug. 1789, cr. EARL OF CARYSFORT, and d. 7 April 1828.
17. 1794, Dec. 12.(e) Charles (Loftus, formerly Tottenham), 1st EARL OF ELY, vice the Earl of Westmeath [No. 4]. He was, on 29 Dec. 1800, cr. MARQUESS OF ELY, and d. 22 March 1806.
18. 1795, March 30.(e) Walter Henry (Fortescue), EARL OF CLERMONT, vice the Earl of Bective [No. 14]. He was invested by the Sovereign in England. He d. 30 Sep. 1806.
19. 1798, March 19.(e) Walter (Butler), EARL OF ORMONDE AND OSSORY, vice the Marquess of Clanricarde [No. 3]. He was, on 12 Jan. 1816, cr. MARQUESS OF ORMONDE. He d. 10 Aug. 1820.
20. „ „(e) Charles (Dillon), 12th VISCOUNT DILLON OF COSTELLO GALLEN, vice the Earl of Clanbrassill [No. 9]. He d. 9 Nov. 1813.
21. 1800, Aug. 5.(e) John Denis (Browne), 3d EARL OF ALTAMONT, vice the Earl of Charlemont [No. 13]. He was, 12 January 1800, cr. MARQUESS OF SLIGO and d. 2 Jan. 1809.

Knights nominated since the Union.

22. 1801, Jan. 22.(f) Henry (Conyngham), 1st EARL CONYNGHAM, vice the Marquess of Waterford [No. 7]. He was, on 22 Jan. 1816, cr. MARQUESS CONYNGHAM, and d. 28 Dec. 1832.
23. 1806, March 14.(f) Henry de la Poer (Beresford), 2d MARQUESS OF WATERFORD vice the Duke of Leinster [No. 2]. He died 16 July 1826.

(b) He was the survivor of the orig. Knights *then existing* as such, the Marquess Wellesley, who survived him 21 years, having resigned in 1810.
(c) He d. 26 Sep. 1842, aged 82, being (by 21 years), the survivor of the original Knights of this order, tho', at his death, not one of them.
(d) Nominated on the refusal of the Earl of Antrim—see, last page, note "a."
(e) Installed at the second installation (of 6 Knights) on 11th Aug. 1800.
(f) Installed at the third installation (of seven Knights) 29 June 1809.

24. 1806, May 15.([f]) Thomas (Taylour), 1st MARQUESS OF HEADFORT, *vice* the Marquess of Ely [No. **17**]. *Invested* by the Sovereign in England. He *d.* 23 Oct. 1829.

25. „ Nov. 13.([f]) Robert (Jocelyn), 2d EARL OF RODEN, *vice* the Earl of Clermont [No. **8**] He *d* 29 June 1820.

26. 1807, Nov. 3.([f]) John (Loftus), 2d MARQUESS OF ELY, *vice* the Earl of Shannon [No. **8**]. He *d.* 23 Sep. 1845.

27. 1808, Sep. 5.([f]) Henry (Boyle), 3rd EARL OF SHANNON, *vice* the Marquess of Thomond [No. **5**]. He *d.* 22 April 1842.

28. 1809, Feb. 13.([f]) Charles Henry St. John (O'Neill), 1st EARL O'NEILL, *vice* the Marquess of Sligo [No. **21**]. He *d.* 25 March 1841.

29. „ Nov. 11.([s]) William (O'Brien), 2nd MARQUESS OF THOMOND, *vice* the Earl of Arran [No. **11**]. He *d.* 21 Aug. 1846.

30. 1810 March 24.([s]) Howe Peter (Browne), 2nd MARQUESS OF SLIGO, *vice* the Marquess Wellesley [No. **10**], resigned. Was *invested*, by spec. dispensation, at Malta. He *d.* 26 Jan. 1845.

31. „ April 27.([s]). John Willoughby (Cole), 2nd EARL OF ENNISKILLEN, *vice* the Earl of Courtown [No. **12**]. He *d.* 31 March 1840.

32. 1813, Dec. 17.([s]) Thomas (Pakenham), 2nd EARL OF LONGFORD, *vice* Viscount Dillon [No. **20**]. He *d.* 24 May 1835.

33. 1821, Aug. 20.([h]) *H.R.H.* Ernest Augustus, DUKE OF CUMBERLAND AND TEVIOTDALE [G.B.] and EARL OF ARMAGH, *vice H.R.H.* the Duke of Kent [No. **1**]. Was *invested*, by proxy, by the Sovereign who was then in Ireland. He became KING OF HANOVER, on 20 June 1837, and *d.* 18 Nov. 1851.

34. „ „([h]) George Augustus (Chichester), 2nd MARQUESS OF DONEGALL, *vice* the Earl of Roden [No. **25**]. He *d.* 5 Oct. 1844.

35. „ „([h]) Du Pre (Alexander), 2nd EARL OF CALEDON, *vice* the Marquess of Ormonde [No. **19**]. He *d.* 8 April 1839.

Six Knights extraordinary were nominated at the Coronation (19 July 1821) of George IV., to be gradually absorbed among the Knights in ordinary, *viz.*

36. „ „([h]) Charles Chetwynd (Talbot), 3rd EARL TALBOT [G.B.], at that time Viceroy of Ireland. He became a *Knight in ordinary, vice* the Marquess of Drogheda, [No. **6**], dec'd. 22 Dec. 1821. He *resigned*, 11 Oct. 1844, on being elected **K.G.**([i])

37. „ „([h]) James (Butler) EARL OF ORMONDE AND OSSORY, who, on 29 Oct. 1825 was *cr.* MARQUESS OF ORMONDE. He became a *Knight in ordinary, vice* the Marquess of Waterford [No. **23**] decd. 16 July, 1826. He *d.* 18 May 1838.

38. „ „([h]) James Chambre (Brabazon), 10th EARL OF MEATH. He became a *Knight in ordinary, vice* the Earl of Carysfort [No. **16**] decd. 7 April 1828. He *d.* 15 March 1851.

39. „ „([h]) Arthur James (Plunkett), 8th EARL OF FINGALL. He became a *Knight in ordinary, vice* the Marquess of Headfoot [No. **24**] decd. 20 Oct. 1829. He *d.* 30 July 1836.

40. „ „([h]) James George (Stopford), 3rd EARL OF COURTOWN. He became a *Knight in ordinary, vice* the Marquess Conyngham [No. **22**] decd. 28 Dec. 1832. He *d.* 15 June 1835.

41. „ „([h]) Robert (Jocelyn), 3rd EARL OF RODEN. He became a *Knight in ordinary* by the statute of 24 Jan. 1833. He *d.* 20 March 1870.

([f]) Installed at the third installation (of seven Knights) 29 June 1809.

([s]) Installed at the fourth installation (of four Knights) 27 May 1819.

([h]) Installed at the fifth installation (of nine Knights) 28 Aug. 1821, the Sovereign himself (who was then in Ireland) being present; the Duke of Cumberland (represented by Thomas, Lord Graves) being installed by proxy.

([i]) He *d.* 13 Jan. 1849. Earl Talbot was the first person, not an *Irish* Peer, who was Knight of this order. The next was, after an interval of thirty years (2), *H.R.H.*

Four Knights extraordinary were nominated at the Coronation [8 Sep. 1831] of William IV., to be gradually absorbed among the Knights in ordinary, *viz.*

42.	1831, Nov. 24.(*k*)	Arthur Blundell Sandys Trumbull (Hill), 2nd MARQUESS OF DOWNSHIRE. He became a *Knight in ordinary* by the statute of 24 Jan. 1833. He *d.* 12 April 1845.
43.	„ Oct. 19(*k*)	Ulick John (de Burgh), 1st MARQUESS OF CLANRICARDE, *invested* by the Sovereign at St. James Palace, England. He became a *Knight in ordinary* by the statute of 24 Jan. 1833. He *d.* 10 April 1874.
44.	„ „(*k*)	Francis William (Caulfield), 2nd EARL OF CHARLEMONT, *invested* as above. He became a *Knight in ordinary* by the statute of 24 Jan. 1833. He *d.* 26 Dec. 1863.
45.	„ Nov. 24(*k*)	Francis James (Mathew), 2nd EARL OF LLANDAFF. He became a *Knight in ordinary* by the statute of 24 Jan. 1833. He *d.* 12 March 1833.

On 24 Jan. 1833 it was enacted that the number of Knights should consist of 22 in lieu of 15 ; the five extraordinary Knights then existing, [Nos. 41 to 45] as above, forming part of that number ; the two vacant posts thus created being filled [by Nos. 46 and 47] as under :—

46.	1833, March 27.	Francis Nathaniel (Conyngham), 2nd MARQUESS CONYNGHAM. By the increase of the order under the statute of 24 Jan. 1833. He *d.* 17 July 1876.
47.	1834, April 8.	Nathaniel (Clements), 8th EARL OF LEITRIM. By the increase of the order under the statute of 24 Jan. 1833. He *d.* 31 Dec. 1854.
48.	„ „	John Hely (Hutchinson), 3rd EARL OF DONOUGHMORE, *vice* the Earl of Llandaff [No. 45]. He *d.* 14 Sep. 1851.
49.	1835, July 22.	Edmund (Boyle) 8th EARL OF CORK and 8th EARL OF ORRERY, *vice* the Earl of Longford [No. 32], *invested* by the Sovereign at St. James, England. He *d.* 30 June 1856.
50.	„ „	Thomas (St. Lawrence), 3rd EARL OF HOWTH, *vice* the Earl of Courtown [No. 40], *invested* as above. He *d.* 4 Feb. 1874.
51.	1837, Sep. 12.	Thomas Anthony (Southwell), 3rd VISCOUNT SOUTHWELL, *vice* the Earl of Fingall [No. 39]. He *d.* 20 Feb. 1860.
52.	1839, April 15.	Thomas (Taylour), 2nd MARQUESS OF HEADFORT, *vice* the Marquess of Ormonde [No. 37]. He *d.* 6 Dec. 1870.
53.	„ „ 29.	William (Hare), 3rd EARL OF LISTOWEL, *vice* the Earl of Caledon [No. 53]. He *d.* 3 Feb. 1856.
54.	1841, March 13.	Joseph (Leeson), 4th EARL OF MILLTOWN, *vice* the Earl of Enniskillen [No. 31]. He *d.* 31 Jan. 1866.
55.	„ May 6.(*l*)	Philip Yorke (Gore), 4th EARL OF ARRAN, *vice* Earl O'Neill [No. 28]. He *d.* 25 June 1884.

the Duke of Cambridge in 1851 ; then (3) Viscount Gough in 1857 ; (4) Baron Lurgan, 1864 ; (5) the Duke of Manchester in 1877 ; (6) Baron O'Hagan and (7) Baron Carlingford, both in 1882 (8) Baron Aunaly (9) Baron Monteagle of Brandon and (10) Viscount Wolseley, all three in 1885. The above is *exclusive* of such members of the Royal family as have been elected *supernumary* Knight, *i.e.* (1) The Prince Consort in 1842 ; (2) The Prince of Wales in 1868 ; (3) Prince Arthur (afterwards Duke of Connaught) in 1869, and (4) the Duke of Edinburgh, in 1880.

(*k*) A Royal warrant, 30 Jan. 1833, dispensed with the installation of these Knights; since which date the installation of all the succeeding Knights (in ordinary) has been similarly dispensed with. The investiture of the 24 Nov. was (as ordinary) by the Grand Master, in Dublin.

(*l*) The dates thus far are from Sir Harris Nicolas' magnificent work, *Orders of Knighthood of the British Empire, &c.*

56. 1842, Jan. 20.(m) *H.R.H.* Francis ALBERT Augustus Charles Emanuel, DUKE OF SAXONY, PRINCE OF SAXE-COBURG AND GOTHA, **K.G.**, &c., declared, by sign manual, an extra Knight, with precedence above all other Knights and dispensation from investiture and installation. He was, on 25 June 1857, cr. PRINCE CONSORT, and *d.* 14 Dec. 1861.

57. „ June 5. William (Howard), EARL OF WICKLOW, *vice* the Earl of Shannon [No. **27**]. He *d.* 22 March 1869.

58. 1845, Jan. 4. William (Parsons), 3rd EARL OF ROSSE, *vice* the Marquess of Donegall [No. **34**]. He *d.* 31 Oct. 1867.

59. „ „ Henry de la Poer (Beresford), 3rd MARQUESS OF WATERFORD, *vice* Earl Talbot [No. **36**], *resigned.* He *d.* 29 March 1859.

60. „ Sep. 17. John (Fitz Gibbon), 2nd EARL OF CLARE, *vice* the Marquess of Sligo [No. **30**]. He *d.* 18 Aug. 1851.

61. „ „ John (Butler), 2nd MARQUESS OF ORMONDE, *vice* the Marquess of Downshire [No. **42**]. He *d.* 25 Sep. 1851.

62. „ Nov. 12. Henry (Maxwell), 7th BARON FARNHAM, *vice* the Marquess of Ely [No. **26**]. He *d.* 20 Aug. 1868.

63. 1846, Oct. 9. Arthur (James Plunkett), 9th EARL OF FINGALL, *vice* the Marquess of Thomond [No. **29**]. He *d.* 22 April 1869.

64. 1851, July 3. John Skeffington (Foster-Skeffington), VISCOUNT MASSEREENE and VISCOUNT FERRARD, *vice* the Earl of Meath [No. **38**]. He *d.* 28 April 1863.

. „ Nov. 18. *H.R.H.* George William Frederick Charles, DUKE OF CAMBRIDGE, EARL OF TIPPERARY, &c. [U.K.], **K.G.**, &c., *vice* the Earl of Clare [No. **60**]. He was living 1889, being then (and having been since June 1884) *the senior Knight* of this most illustrious order.

66. „ „ Robert Shapland (Carew), 1st BARON CAREW, *vice* the Earl of Donoughmore [No. **48**]. He *d.* 2 June 1856.

67. 1855, Feb. 22. Richard (Dawson), 3rd BARON CREMORNE, *vice* the King of Hanover [No. **33**]. He was on 12 July 1866, cr. EARL OF DARTREY [U.K.] He was living 1889.

68. „ „ Archibald (Acheson), 3rd EARL OF GOSFORD, *vice* the Marquess of Ormonde [No. **61**]. He *d.* 15 June 1864.

69. 1856, Aug. 28. Frederick William Robert (Stewart), 4th MARQUESS OF LONDONDERRY, *vice* the Earl of Leitrim [No. **47**]. He *d.* 25 Nov. 1872.

70 1857, Jan. 30. George Arthur Hastings (Forbes), 7th EARL OF GRANARD, *vice* the Earl of Listowel [No. **53**]. He was living 1889.

71. „ „ Hugh (Gough), 1st VISCOUNT GOUGH OF GOOJERAT AND OF LIMERICK [U.K.],(n) *vice* Baron Carew [No. **66**]. He *d.* 2 March 1869.

72. „ Feb. 3. George Hamilton (Chichester), 3rd MARQUESS OF DONEGALL, *vice* the Earl of Cork [No. **49**]. He *d.* 20 Oct. 1883.

73. 1859, May 24. Arthur Wills Blundell Sandys Trumbull Windsor (Hill), 4th MARQUESS OF DOWNSHIRE, *vice* the Marquess of Waterford [No. **59**]. He *d.* 6 Aug. 1868.

74. 1860, June 13. Richard Edmund St. Lawrence (Boyle), 9th EARL OF CORK and EARL OF ORRERY, *vice* Viscount Southwell [No. **51**]. He was living 1889.

75. 1864, Jan. 28. Frederick Temple (Hamilton-Blackwood), BARON DUFFERIN AND CLANEBOYE, *vice* Viscount Massereene [No. **64**]. He was, on 13 Nov. 1871, cr. EARL OF DUFFERIN [U.K.], and, in Nov. 1888, MARQUESS OF DUFFERIN AND AVA [U.K.] He was living 1889.

(m) The dates from this period are from the " Statutes, &c., of St. Patrick " (printed 1852, with supplement to 1883), edited by Sir J. Bernard Burke, Ulster King of Arms, &c., those since 1883, being kindly supplied by his son, H. Farnham Burke, Somerset Herald.

(n) See two pages back, note " i."

76.	1864, March 31.	Charles (Brownlow), 2nd BARON LURGAN [U.K.],[o] *vice* the Earl of Charlemont [No. 44]. He *d.* 15 Jan. 1882.
77.	1865, Dec. 28.	James Molyneux (Caulfeild), 3rd EARL OF CHARLEMONT, *vice* the Earl of Gosford [No. 68]. He was living 1889.
78.	1866, March 13.	Edwin Richard (Wyndham-Quin), 3rd EARL OF DUNRAVEN AND MOUNTEARL, *vice* the Earl of Milltown [No. 54]. He *d.* 6 Oct. 1871.
79.	1868, Feb. 7.	Henry Francis Seymour (Moore), 3rd MARQUESS OF DROGHEDA, *vice* the Earl of Rosse [No. 58]. He was living 1889.
80.	„ March 18.	*H.R.H.* ALBERT EDWARD, PRINCE OF WALES, K.G., &c., declared by sign manual an extra Knight, with precedence above all other Knights. He was *installed* at St. Patrick's Cathedral, 18 April 1868 and was living 1889.
81.	„ Nov. 17.	John Henry de la Poer (Beresford), 5th MARQUESS OF WATERFORD, *vice* the Marquess of Downshire [No. 73]. He was living 1889.
82.	„ „	John (Crichton), 3rd EARL ERNE, *vice* Baron Farnham [No. 68]. He *d.* 3 Oct. 1885.
83.	„ „ 25.	Richard Southwell (Bourke), 6th EARL OF MAYO, Gov. Gen. of India. He was created *a Knight extraordinary* under sign manual 11 Nov. 1868, but became a *Knight in ordinary*, *vice* Viscount Gough [No. 71] deceased 2 March 1869. He was *invested* at Calcutta. He *d.* 8 Feb. 1872.
84.	1869, March 30.	*H.R.H.* Prince ARTHUR William Patrick Albert, K.G., &c., declared by sign manual an extra Knight, with precedence next to the Prince of Wales. He was, on 28 May 1874, *cr.* DUKE OF CONNAUGHT AND STRATHEARN [U.K.], and was living 1889.
85.	„ June 2.	Granville Leveson (Proby), 4th EARL OF CARYSFORT, *vice* the Earl of Wicklow [No. 57]. He *d.* 18 May 1872.
86.	„ „	Archibald Brabazon Sparrow (Acheson), 4th EARL OF GOSFORD, *vice* the Earl of Fingall [No. 63]. He was living 1889.
87.	1871, Aug. 2.	Mervyn (Wingfield), 7th VISCOUNT POWERSCOURT, *vice* the Earl of Roden [No. 41]. He was living 1889.
88.	„ „	Thomas Arthur Joseph (Southwell), 4th VISCOUNT SOUTHWELL, *vice* the Marquess of Headfort [No. 52]. He *d.* 26 April 1878.
89.	1872, Feb. 29.	Robert Shapland (Carew), 2nd BARON CAREW, *vice* the Earl of Dunraven and Mountearl [No. 78]. He *d.* 9 Sep. 1881.
90.	„ June 1.	Valentine Augustus (Browne), 4th EARL OF KENMARE, *vice* the Earl of Mayo [No. 83]. He was living 1889.
91.	1873, Feb. 20.	William (Hare), 3rd EARL OF LISTOWEL, *vice* the Earl of Carysfort [No. 85]. He was living 1889.
92.	1874, Aug. 31.	William (Proby), 5th EARL OF CARYSFORT, *vice* the Marquess of Londonderry [No. 69]. He was living 1889.
93.	„ „	George Henry Robert Charles William (Vane-Tempest), 5th MARQUESS OF LONDONDERRY, *vice* the Earl of Howth [No. 50]. He *d.* 6 Nov. 1884.
94.	1876, May 13.	Windham Thomas (Wyndham-Quin), 4th EARL OF DUNRAVEN AND MOUNTEARL, *vice* the Marquess of Clanricarde [No. 43]. He was living 1889.
95.	1877, March 3.	William Drogo (Montagu), 7th DUKE OF MANCHESTER [G.B.],[o] *vice* the Marquess Conyngham [No. 46]. He was living 1889.
96.	1879, Feb. 8.	Henry John Reuben (Dawson-Damer), 3rd EARL OF PORTARLINGTON, *vice* Viscount Southwell [No. 88]. He was living 1889.
97.	1880, May 20.	*H.R.H.* Alfred Ernest Albert, DUKE OF EDINBURGH, EARL OF KENT, AND EARL OF ULSTER [U.K.]. K.G., &c., declared by

(o) See three pages back, note "i."

		sign manual an extra Knight, with precedence next to the Prince of Wales. He was living 1889.
98.	1882, Jan. 17.	Thomas (O'Hagan), 1st BARON O'HAGAN OF TULLAHOGUE [U.K.],P and late Lord Chancellor of Ireland ; *vice* Baron Carew [No. 89]. He *d.* 1 Feb. 1885.
99.	„ April 11.	Chichester Samuel (Parkinson-Fortescue), BARON CARLINGFORD [U.K.],P *vice* Baron Lurgan [No. 76]. He suc., 27 July 1887, to an Irish Peerage, as BARON CLERMONT, and was living 1889.
100.	1884, May 8.	William Ulick Tristram (St. Lawrence), 4th EARL OF HOWTH, *vice* the Marquess of Donegall [No. 72]. He was living 1889.
101.	1885, Feb. 9.	Luke (White), 2nd BARON ANNALY [U.K.],P *vice* the Earl of Arran [No. 55]. He *d.* 16 March 1888.
102.	„ „	Thomas Spring (Rice), 2nd BARON MONTEAGLE OF BRANDON [U.K.],P *vice* the Marquess of Londonderry [No. 94]. He and all subsequently elected Knights were living 1889.
103.	„ Nov. 28.	Garnet Joseph (Wolseley) VISCOUNT WOLSELEY, [U.K.],P *vice* Baron O'Hagan [No. 98].
104.	„ „	Thomas (Taylour), 3rd MARQUESS OF HEADFORT, *vice* Earl Erne [No. 82].
105.	1887, June 28.	*H.R.H. Prince* ALBERT VICTOR Christian Edward, K.G., 1st son of *H.R.H.* the PRINCE OF WALES, declared by sign manual an extra Knight.
106.	1888, April 26.	James Edward William Theobald (Butler), 3rd MARQUESS OF ORMONDE, *vice* Baron Annaly [No. 101].

(P) See four pages back, note ' i."

INDEX TO THE PEERAGE OF IRELAND,

As contained in the above ten tables.

The Roman numerals, I to X, refer to the tables so numbered, after which is, in this index, placed the *date*, every *date* in each such table being in strict *chronological* order. The abbreviation "Visc." is here used, instead of "V" (as used in the tables themselves) for "Viscount," so as not to make confusion with the *numeral* "V," which in this index, refers to "*Table* V ;" the letters " D.," " M.," " E.," and " B." stand (as in the tables) for "Duke," "Marquess," "Earl," and "Baron."

The Peerage titles *within square brackets* are peerages of England, Great Britain, or the United Kingdom, held by any Irish Peer, at or since the Union (as given in Table VIII), or by those few noblemen who, *not* being Irish Peers, or holding an Irish Peerage of *inferior* grade, have been made (as in Table X) Knights of St. Patrick. The *surnames* of Peers are printed *in italics*.

It should be noted that it is not *every* peerage title *of inferior rank* existing at or since the Union that is in the index, but only such as are in the tables themselves. Thus the Barony of Cloumore (1776), tho' the peerage of *greatest antiquity* held by the Earl of Wicklow, is *not* herein, inasmuch as, its creation being *subsequent* to the accession of George III, it is *not* in Table II ; so also as to the Viscounty of Duncannon (1722), an inferior title, but *not* the one of greatest antiquity, held by the Earl of Bessborough ; so also with the Earldom of Belfast (1791), the Viscounty of Carlingford (*cr.* 1761 ; *ex.* 1853), peerages conferred in the *same patent* as the Marquessate of Donegall and the Earldom of Tyrconnel respectively.

It may be convenient to insert here a *synopsis* of each table thus referred to in this Index, *viz.:*—

TABLE	I.	Peerages existing at or since the Union, under the title of the Peerage *highest in rank.*
TABLE	II.	Peerages existing at the Union, *anterior to the accession of George III,* under the date of the peerage of *greatest antiquity.*
TABLE	III.	Peerages held at the Union by *Females.*
TABLE	IV.	Peerages *extinct* since the Union, including those held by the same person of which the patents were distinct.
TABLE	V.	Peerages existing separately at the time of the Union, but since *merged* into higher or more ancient titles.
TABLE	VI.	Peerages made *by creation* since the Union.
TABLE	VII.	Peerages made *by promotion* since the Union.
TABLE	VIII.	Peerages united with Peerages of *England, Great Britain,* or *the United Kingdom,* at or since the Union.
TABLE	IX.	Peerages held by *Representative* Peers, since the Union.
TABLE	X.	Peerages held by *Knights of St. Patrick,* since 1783, the date of the institution of that order.

(a) Albert Edward, Prince of Wales, was cr. Earl of Dublin [U.K.] in 1850 ; but

---

(ᵃ) George Fitz Clarence, illegit. son of the above (afterwards, 1830, William IV. was cr., in 1831, Earl of Munster *in the United Kingdom*.

(ᵃ) H.R.H. Prince Alfred was *cr.* Duke of Edinburgh, *Earl of Ulster* [U.K.] &c., in 1866.

Wicklow (*Howard*), E., I and III, 1793;
IX, 1801, 1821, 1872, 1888; X, (K.P.)
1842; Visc., I, 1785; |IX, 1801 ; V,
1807.
Wingfield, see Powerscourt.
Winn, see Headley.
Winterton (*Turnour*), E., I, 1766.
Wolfe, see Kilwarden.
[*Wolseley*, see Wolseley.]
[Wolseley (*Wolseley*), Visc., X (K.P.)
1885.]

[Worlingham (*Acheson*), B., cr. 1835, see
Gosford, E., VIII, 1835.]
[Wycombe (*Fitzmaurice-Petty*), B., cr.
1760 ; see Shelburne, E., VIII, 1760.]
Wynn, see Newborough.

Yelverton, see Avonmore.
[York (*Prince Frederick*), D., cr. 1784 ;
cx. 1827 ; see Ulster, E., I and VIII,
1874.]

ERRATA ET ADDENDA.

TABLE I. under " EARLS," after "1793 " insert " 1794 " before " *Macartney*."
    "   "   " for " 1806, Blessington" read " 1816, Blesington," and
       transpose accordingly.
    "   "   " under the date "1822" transpose "Listowel" and "Dunraven."
    "   " " VISCOUNTS,"   "   "1775, Mountjoy," for " pr. 1806 " read
       " pr. 1816."
    "   "   " for " 1802, *Newcomen* " read " 1803, *Newcomen*."
    "   "   " for " 1815, Frankfort " read " 1816, Frankfort."
    "   "   " between " Frankfort " and " Gort " insert,
" 1816, *Mountearl* (see Barony of Adare, cr. 1980) pr. 1822 to the Earldom of Dunraven.
1816, *Ennismore and Listowel* (see Barony of Ennismore, cr. 1800) pr. 1822 to the
       Earldom of Listowel.
TABLE I. under "BARONS," for " 1585, Caher " read " 1583, Caher."
    "   "   " after " 1620 " insert " 1621 " as the date for " Blayney."
    "   "   " under " 1800 " insert after " Adare " the words " pr. 1816
       to the Viscountcy of Mountearl."
    "   "   " under " 1800 " insert after " Ennismore " the words " pr.
       1816, to the Viscountcy of Ennismore."
TABLE II. for " 1550 " read " 1541 " ; for " 1626 " read '1616 " ; for " 1629 " read
    " 1619," and for " 1715 " read 1717," as the respective
       dates of the creations of the Baronies of " Dunboyne,"
       " Brabazon," " Kilkenny West," and " Brodrick."
TABLE IV. under " 1814," for " 1773 " read " 1738," before " Bellfield."
TABLE VIII. for " 1816 " read " 1815," before " Limerick."
    "   insert between " 1815 " and " 1821,"
" 1818 | Kerry, E. (*Fitzmaurice*), cr. 1722 | Lansdowne, M., cr. 1784 | 19 | (d) | "
Alter numbers " 19 "—" 78 " in fourth column to " 20 "—" 79," and add note " d,"
as under, " By the death of the Earl of Kerry in 1818, that Earldom devolved on
the Earl of Shelburne, who was Marquess of Lansdowne [U.K.] See in this Table
under 1760."
After " 1825 " read " 1826," before " Thomond," " Clanricarde," and "Northland."
Under " 1850," insert in third column, after " Dufferin, E., cr. 1871," the words
" Dufferin, and Ava, M., cr. 1888."

FINIS.